Jesus and the Goddess

Living into a ChristoPagan theology

Table of Contents

Beginning and the End 163

Suggested Reading 164

Appendix One: The Rosary and other Prayers 176

Dedication

To Michael and Robert,

with all my love.

In memory of our son, Nicodemus.

Introduction

This book, like any other, is a labor of love. As a student of religion, I have become convinced that one of the emerging themes of the 21st century is the blending of things that were once separated into distinct categories. From family to music, from ethnicity to religion, boundaries are being crossed as never before.[i] It is my hope that this book provides an exploration of the ways in which two religions, usually considered anathema to each other, can actually be blended in a way that can provide deep spiritual meaning and guidance to practitioners.

This book is one of the first on the subject, and as such it is my hope that this work will open a door for many to follow behind me, making this path their own. This book is my explanation of my connection. I have had personal spiritual experiences that have convinced me of the power of the Divine in Pagan rituals, while at the same time I have been confronted with the reality that for me, Christ is a central presence in my life and my relationship with Him alters all I am and do. So for me, with my life experiences, there was no question of rejecting one or the other, rather I have been on a quest to make sense of my experiences with both religions, and through prayer and practice I have developed the system and theology presented here. I am not claiming to have the One True Way, nor am I claiming that this book is the final word on the subject. I know that I am a product of my time, culture, language, and religious past and as such, I cannot say that I have seen *the* face of God, only that I have seen the face of God for myself. In other words, this book is a starting point, not (I trust) my final contribution to the subject.

My desire in writing this is was not to reinvent the wheel, but to prove that this way of blending faiths can be done, with respect and sensitivity, acknowledging that there are difficulties but also acknowledging that there are very real benefits to doing so. I do not wish to convert anyone or to proselytize, I believe that each person must find their own way to become more loving. What I do wish to do is offer my path as one example of how religion can become a gateway to inclusion and diversity, instead of something that divides people. If you are like me, called to two religions (for whatever reasons) and unwilling to reject either one, then I hope this book will help you in your search. Take what works, ignore what does not, and whatever you do, do it in love! I hope this work inspires your own spiritual journey, and I look forward to hearing from you about your spiritual explorations.

Central Premise

The central premise of this book is important enough to warrant a special place at the beginning. Simply put, I believe that every religion has *Something or Someone that MUST be seriously addressed*. For me, this Something or Someone is the defining feature of that religion. That Something or Someone is not, however, something that is central to or even usually a focus of another faith. For example, to be Buddhist, one must delve into the teachings of the Buddhist canon. A Jewish person does not need to ever think about the Buddha to be a good Jew. They might do so, but it is not required for their faith. This Someone or Something is not the only facet of a religion, but it is the irreducible central element that the faith revolves around. Based on that idea, in this book, I am defining Christianity and Paganism as follows:

To be Christian, you MUST seriously address Jesus and the Bible. To be Pagan you MUST seriously address the Earth and the Divine Feminine.

By seriously I simply mean that these are elements of the faith that must be addressed, not as things with one answer or approach. When you look at religions, each one has a wide umbrella of ways to authentically belong to the community. There are devout Christians who see Jesus as the literal Son of God; there are devout Christians who see Jesus as an inspired example of faith, but not super-human. My premise is that while people often disagree about what makes a "true" Christian, in order to be a part of the discussion a person must discuss Jesus and the Bible. A person wishing to be a Christian scholar who never talked about the Bible or about Jesus would not be taken seriously by Christianity.

The same idea applies to Paganism. Wiccans, Druids, New Age practitioners, Eclectic Circles, Solitary Practitioners, and Asatru[ii] (among others) can all fall under the heading of "Pagan", although all of them disagree strongly on many theological points. However, in all Pagan groups I am aware of, discussions of the Earth and discussions of the Divine are important aspects of the faith. Even if the group does not have a theistic god figure, such as in humanistic Paganism, the topic of the Divine is addressed.[iii]

Having made my claim, I feel the need to point out that my schema for quantifying religion is not the be all and end all of a faith. It is, instead, a starting point for my explorations. When blending religious traditions, a question that must be asked is what is non-negotiable. What is it that *must* remain or else you have lost the essence of the faith. For me, this is the Someone or Something of that faith. Please note that this schema, and this book, are but a starting point for theology.

What is ChristoPaganism?

ChristoPaganism is an emerging 21st century syncretic religious tradition which blends elements from both Christian and Pagan practice to create a life of meaning for adherents. Syncretic religions grow from the lived experiences of their practitioners, adding and subtracting elements of belief, doctrine, and practice to meet the needs of the community. All religions do this to some extent or another, but syncretic religions focus on harmonizing two or more religions to meet these needs. In ChristoPagan practice, people have found meaning in both Paganism and in Christianity, two religions that have a long history of being antagonistic. Despite this antagonism at the institutional level, for some people neither faith alone satisfies, but the combination of both provides a way to make meaning and encourage personal growth.

If you are one of these people, then this book is written for you. I present my own, sometimes rambling, thoughts on the major doctrines of Christianity and Paganism, seeking ways to blend both of these that address both my need to express my experience and my need to have a rational system of belief. I do not ask anyone to believe that this is the only way to synthesize these two great religious traditions, but for anyone seeking a guide to help them harmonize the major differences between these faiths, I hope this work will serve as at least a basic map for how to go about the process for yourself.

Theological Method

How we come to believe is as important, in many ways, as what we end up believing. The method I was taught in seminary offers four avenues for the development of theology: scripture, reason (scientific inquiry), tradition and experience.[iv] There are other methods for theological reflection, but this has the advantage of being simple, and it is the one I personally use although I have adapted it extensively.

One of the adaptations I have made is to see this as the starting point, not the final word. I believe that good theology should include all four points, but which point is primary changes with the theological perspective of the individual. More conservative churches use either tradition or Scripture as the start, everything must be justified through one of those before it can be accepted by the church. More mainline and liberal churches use reason and personal experience in the same way, editing the Bible and the tradition of the church to fit new cultural and scientific developments.

For ChristoPagans, syncretism is the core of the faith, meaning that it begins from the perspective of personal experience and then decides from that point what traditions, beliefs, and Scripture will be included. This is good because it allows the faith to grow and change, but it has great potential for it to get bogged down in arguments of experience, or to be hijacked by charismatic people who can pressure others into deeming their experiences more valid. There is tension in all theology, between experiences of something far beyond our rational selves and the need to quantify this experience in finite words. This tension is even greater when experience leads a person to a place where they must sort through and make sense of traditions which are generally antithetical to one another.

A solid theological method helps with this process by aiding the faithful in sorting through what they believe, why and how, and connecting that to the larger traditions they come from. The process used here is simple. For each doctrine, personal experience provides the initial insight.

Next, the traditions of the faith are consulted to find where this can connect to the parent traditions. Modern science (the 'reason' part) is not rejected, but mined for important insights and corrections to experience and tradition. Finally, Scripture is consulted to make sure that a particular doctrine has at least some grounding in Biblical interpretation.

To illustrate this process, I have personally experienced God through elemental rituals. By consulting the traditions of Christianity and Paganism, I find that there are branches of Christianity where the Earth was honored as a manifestation of God, and that an entire branch of theology (Creation Spirituality) follows this lead. Paganism, of course, reveres the Earth more than almost any other faith. Science offers a variety of ways to understand how I am connected to the Earth, along with millions of reasons to care about the planet and my place in it. Finally, there are lots of Bible studies about the Earth and varying interpretations of how God manifests in and through the material world. Thus, by following the theological method of Experience, Tradition, Reason, and Scripture, I am able to understand how my experience fits into a larger Christian or ChristoPagan theology.

For each doctrine in this book, the same process was followed, although it is not explicitly pointed out in every case. Where experiences differ, the rest of the conclusion will differ, because experience is the starting point for this theological reflection. It does not mean that either conclusion is abjectly wrong, just that they started from different places and drew from different parts of the tradition.

Each ChristoPagan participates in not one but two millennia old traditions of faith, systems for making meaning of the world. Every person experiences life in a way utterly unique to them, so having some common understanding of how we describe experiences in theological terms, and where in the tradition we draw from, can help us not only discuss our faith, but find others of like mind who draw from the same historical teachings as we do.

Central tenets

How this book is organized

This book looks at central tenets of both faiths, and each topic follows a standardized format. While they are designed to be read start to finish, this standard format allows the reader to browse by topic if they so choose. The format for each topic is as follows:

- The "traditional" Christian understanding

- The "traditional" Pagan understanding

- The arguments against blending the Christian and Pagan understandings

- Suggested theology for blending Christian and Pagan understandings

Both of these religious traditions are vast, and as such, in order to keep this work on the level of an introduction and not bog down the contents with thousands of years of theological writing, when I reference the "traditional" view I am generally referring to the "popular" or "common" understanding in America as portrayed via the Internet, "basic" books on the subject (such as can be found at large chain bookstores), and my own experiences talking to people as a theologian and pastor. I realize that each and every topic has a plethora of understandings and views, and there is simply not room to list them all.

I have tried to choose understandings that are both liberal and conservative, in keeping with the nature of this chapter, and filtered through the situations practitioners of ChristoPaganism are likely to face when dealing with family, friends, and religious groups. Where I could, I have cited the Internet primarily as a recognition of the fact that few people have access to all the theological tomes I have acquired through seminary and beyond. However, I am also including a list of Suggested Reading by topic at the end of this book should you feel the need to tackle any of the subjects here in more depth. This work is informed by scholarship, but since I am primarily writing for faithful people, not religious scholars, there is a great deal of non-academic material cited here as well. While the Internet can give you a feeling for the breadth of material, I do not advocate any site or group, (and many of them would never advocate me) nor do I confine my study to the Internet. The Internet, like this book, is a starting point for dialogue, nothing more.

I speak and write as a progressive Christian, born and raised in Christian denominations, steeped in Christian theology from undergraduate to seminary and into my doctoral work. I am but a late comer to Paganism, (primarily through eclectic Pagan groups, which are but one expression of Pagan religion), and as such, this work is more heavily slanted toward making ChristoPaganism more understandable to Christians or those coming from a dominant Christian culture like America. I do not delve into Esoteric Christianity, although many ChristoPagans including myself find a great deal of value in the study of non-mainstream Christian theologies. However, the mystical traditions tend to place more weight on direct linage-style teaching, while I wanted to write a book that people without my background could follow.

Modern Paganism is still developing doctrinally and theologically, and as a practical matter, it is more likely that a ChristoPagan will meet with more Christians than Pagans, since Christianity is still the dominant religious culture in America.[v] For these reasons, I do not dwell as deeply on Pagan theology (although I do try to give it thoughtful attention).

Finally, while I think I have addressed the major topics of faith in both religions, there may very well be areas I left untouched. If you have a burning question about how to blend an area of faith I left out of this work, contact me (information is at the end of the book) and I will do my best to provide an answer. Remember, this is the beginning of the dialog, not my (or God's) final say on anything! *Amen and Blessed Be.*

God

- The "traditional" Christian understanding

The traditional Christian understanding of God is that of the Trinity.[vi] God is eternal (outside/beyond time) and both transcendent (separate from the world) and immanent (present within the world). God exists as a three-in-one entity named by the early Christian church as Father, Son, and Spirit. All three members of the Trinity are mystically One, even as they are Three. How, exactly, this occurs is the source of much debate and even schism in the Christian church, and it remains problematic to this day. In fact, the doctrine of the Trinity is so complex and confusing that attempts to simplify it often lead to 'heretical' understandings.[vii]

A simple and common understanding of the Trinity that many Christians hold is that God the Father is the creator of the finite world, and exists beyond it in heaven. God the Son came into the world to save us from our sins, but ascended to heaven after his death and resurrection. God the Spirit is the ongoing work of God (and/or Jesus) in the world today, either as the sponsor of the Church or in direct contact with individuals.[viii]

Various debates and schisms have occurred over the hierarchy of the members of the Trinity, including the split between Western and Eastern Christianity over the *filioque* clause added to the Nicene Creed (the question was if the Holy Spirit was equal or subordinate to Jesus, with Eastern and Western churches in disagreement).[ix] Jesus is seen as the second member of the Trinity, either in an upside-down pyramid with he and God the Father at the top and the Spirit beneath (Western view), or in a typical pyramid with God the Father at the top and Jesus and the Spirit sharing the lower tier (Eastern view). Debate over this topic caused the split between Eastern (Orthodox) and Western (Roman Catholic, and later Protestant) churches that continues to exist even today.

Historically, dedication to the Trinity has rarely been uniform; today many churches focus on Jesus largely to the exclusion of the Father and

Spirit, while Charismatic churches focus on the Spirit more than the Father and Son. Modern feminist theologians are reclaiming the feminine side of the Divine, a view of the Trinity that will be explored more in the "blending" section. However, one common theme in Christian understandings of the Divine is that we are not God. We may, through God's grace, participate in God, but we are not divine in and of ourselves.

- The "traditional" Pagan understanding

Pagan understandings of God/dess are as varied as Paganism itself. Typical understandings range from polytheism (many gods, which may or may not be manifestations of one Source); to pantheism (God is nature); to panentheism (God dwells within, but is also more than, nature). An emerging understanding is Humanistic, that is, a Paganism which rejects the supernatural and seeks to live an ethical life based on human understandings, not seeking Divine revelation. Some Pagan traditions focus on a specific historical pantheon of deities for rituals and worship while others simply worship the God and Goddess, just the Goddess, or even just the Earth.[x]

Virtually any book on Paganism will list deities and correspondences for worship, and even traditions which focus on a particular deity or pantheon will rarely make the claim that theirs is the only manifestation of God/dess. There is a range of acceptance of deity forms, from the hard polytheists who know that there are lots of gods and that believing anything else is wrong, to the individualists who think we create the divine through our thought-processes. In the middle are those 'soft polytheists' who feel that while the aspects of the Divine that they worship may have distinct forms or ways of being, they are probably part of a larger Source of divinity.[xi]

- The arguments against blending the Christian and Pagan understandings

The arguments against blending faith come from the more conservative sides of both faiths. Christians say that God may only be known as the Trinity of Father, Son, and Spirit; while Pagans say that Jesus was a nice person but not God, and that

God can be *triune* but is not limited to that. Hard polytheists say that gods are individuals and that they may not be combined in any way into a larger whole. In many ways this is a kind of Pagan fundamentalism, since they reject understandings that are different from their own. Conservative theology on both sides is indeed quite hostile to the other, with Christians claiming Pagans are going to hell, and Pagans claiming Christians are responsible for the horrors of the past several millennia.[xii] One only has to visit a few websites or read a couple of books to pick up on this hostility. However, liberal or inclusive theology on both sides offers a method for finding a middle ground which gives respect to both, while acknowledging the flaws in each.

- Suggested theology for blending Christian and Pagan understandings

Blending these two faiths seems to me to require a liberal or inclusive approach. Someone who is fundamentalist[xiii] in thought would be hard pressed to justify how anyone else can have any part of the truth. However, remembering that religion is a broad umbrella, there are more tolerant and inclusive views within both Christianity and Paganism that allow for a blending of understandings about God, and there is historical justification for this position.

First, God is not exclusively male. Within the Christian Bible there are times when God is referenced in feminine language, and even the early church saw God's feminine qualities.[xiv] Thus, much of modern fundamentalist Christianity and its insistence on God's maleness (and women having lesser status because of this) is based in poor scholarship, a desire to keep the patriarchal status-quo, and a refusal to read the Bible. Yes, God in the Christian Bible is portrayed as mainly masculine. There is no getting around that fact. However, the fact that there are *any* references to God as female or feminine mean that this is an aspect of God present in Christianity.

Further, an understanding of the historical situation of the Bible informs us that many of the things considered violent or repulsive to us today are in fact products of their time. This way of reading the Bible is dependent on an understanding that while the Bible may be inspired by God, the people who wrote it were flawed beings who were products of their culture and time.[xv] Thus, according to this view, the Bible is a conversation between people and God, subject to changes in culture and understanding. There are many, many good works of scholarship on biblical interpretation, some of which are referenced in the Suggested Reading. The point for this work is that there are different ways to read the Bible, and that in some of those interpretations God can be feminine as well as masculine; a point that Pagans and Christians can agree on.

Second, the Trinity itself is a product of thousands of years of Christian scholarship and thought, and even today the way various denominations teach this doctrine is varied and diverse. The historical teachings of the church give some credence to the idea of God as male and female, masculine and feminine (and even more importantly, that God is emphatically beyond any human category); while varying teachings about the procession of the Trinity open the door for a discussion of how God is made manifest in the world. The idea that God's Spirit infuses creation can lead to a panentheist view of the world, which has already been shown to be in accord with some modes of Pagan thought. Further, the idea that the Spirit of God (especially the Spirit as Feminine) manifests according to Her own design could possibly lead to an understanding of multiple manifestations, each a facet or aspect of the Holy. This idea is how I have bridged the Christian-Pagan divide, and as such it is developed throughout this book.

Historically, religious insistence on One True Way has, in fact, caused needless pain and suffering, death and persecution for those who are different. In fact most of ancient history is based around which gods conquered which parts of the globe. Horrible, terrible, violent things have been and are being done in the name of God (whatever name that was or is) and we should all be ashamed of the ways religion uses God as a tool to propagate agendas of power and violence. Modern Pagans and Christians (and Buddhists and Muslims and everyone else for that matter) need to stop blaming each other for what happened in the past, and need to start working together to ensure that religion is never again used as a tool for violence. This should be a primary goal of all religions, whether or not they have syncretic members.

That said, how can a Pagan theology, especially one where the Divine Feminine is honored, be blended with the Christian Trinity? One suggested method is as follows. First, an acknowledgment that there can be commonalities to the ways Paganism and Christianity view the Divine. Examples include the fact that God/dess is neither exclusively male nor female, but is instead larger than we can imagine. God/dess is loving and nurturing, strong and virulent. God/dess is seen in nature and yet is more than the sum of Her parts. This is a panentheistic way to view the Divine and it blends the two traditions well. In this view, God/dess may be seen at work in and through nature, although God is not limited to that, which can work well for teaching children about God. Jesus even used this method of teaching. Many parables use ordinary things to demonstrate what God is like. *God is like a farmer sowing a field, God is like a woman cleaning her house, God is a mother hen, God is our Rock...*all these are Bible-based images of God.[xvi] For Pagan theologies which allow for God to be larger than the gods of old, God/dess can be seen as variously manifesting to accommodate human needs, and as such Jesus, Mary, etc. can be incorporated into the pantheon of worshiped divine entities quite easily.[xvii]

Second, if the Trinity is conceptualized as God the Father, God the Mother, and God the Child, we can see the parallels to the way the Divine is often discussed in some Pagan theology. For example, at Yule the Goddess gives birth to the Sun God, who returns light to the world. He then becomes Her lover/consort at Beltane, father of all fertility. This restructuring of the Trinity is novel, but I believe it is consistent with the debates over the inner life of the Trinity that have raged for centuries.[xviii] This approach is perhaps the easiest to conceptualize, since it keeps the basic structure of Father, Son, and Spirit, admittedly personifying the Spirit as feminine; and it maintains the family bonds of the Trinity that are an important aspect of the Christian understanding of the Divine.[xix] Further, it is simple to understand without much of the overly complicated language that is often used when dealing with the Trinity.

One problem with this approach is that the Divine Child is seen as male, as Jesus. Does this make the Trinity more male than female? One way of understanding the Incarnation reads it as God giving preference to maleness,[xx] but a more inclusive reading of the Incarnation can acknowledge the fact that at the time of Jesus' birth women were not given voice in their communities, as such if Jesus had come as a woman, she would have never been able to spread the message of love and hope that a man could.[xxi] In this theology, the gender of the Incarnation is less about God's desire or preference for the male, and more about humanity's refusal to give men and women equal place. In this light, the Trinity is balanced between mother/father God and the Incarnate God, the Anointed One we know as Jesus, whose maleness is a result of humanity's problems, not Divine decree. This is an interpretation that fits both with a historical-critical examination of the Bible, and with a theology that sees gender equality as a central element of religious life (more on gender and sexuality later, I promise!). Based on this, we then proceed to a discussion of this mysterious God-yet-human. The role of Jesus is much debated, both inside and outside of Christianity. Primarily the debate is over whether he is God or human, and what role he played in salvation (and as such, what role he continues to play or not play in that today).

Jesus

Jesus is understood in the Christian tradition as the Incarnate Word of God. Son of God, Savior, Prince of Peace; these are but a few of the titles given to him by his later followers.[xxii] Remember back at the beginning of this book the claim that to be Christian one must take Jesus seriously? His role in the Trinity, his role as the Incarnation, and his role as the Savior are all important things to examine within Christian faith, and especially in discussion of a ChristoPagan faith which seeks to respect Christian theology as well as Pagan theology.

To begin at the end, let us examine what it means for Jesus to be the savior. Traditional theology holds that people broke God's law and were distanced from God. This created a separation from God which we were powerless to overcome. God, in mercy, sent Jesus to atone (pay) for our sin. There are six major theories of atonement, ranging from the Ransom Theory (where God bribes Satan to let humanity go), to the Satisfaction Theory (where God is the angry judge that can only be appeased by killing someone, but since no human is good enough, God has to kill His own Son).[xxiii] Many modern scholars have found these theories to be at best, unhelpful and at worst, devastating to faith since God is portrayed as a thief, an arbitrary tyrant, or a child-abuser. Much of liberal Christian theology ignores atonement theory entirely, focusing on the life and actions of Jesus instead.[xxiv] For myself, I think there is a great lesson to be learned from Jesus' life, death, and resurrection in ways that are neither abusive, nor antithetical to Pagan belief and practice.

Jesus is Savior is an ancient Christian creed.[xxv] But what, exactly, are we saved *from*, what are we saved *to*, and *how* are we saved? Every denomination has at least one, and usually several, answers to these questions. Read the official statements of any denomination to learn their particular take(s) on this subject. As ChristoPagans, we are pioneers of an emerging denomination, or at least an emerging theology, and as such we too can provide answers to these questions.

One possible set of answers that takes his life, death, and resurrection seriously is this: **Relationship with Jesus, as a God-Incarnation (*avatar*), saves us from being selfishly centered in ourselves, saves us to a fullness of life wherein we see all things as part of God and we know that we have a place in the life of God, and we are saved through devotional relationship with Jesus and through our own pursuit of our God-nature.**

Breaking this statement down, sin is seen generally as two things. First, the perception that we are separated from the Divine and second, the tragedy of failing to live up to our potential (*hamartia*, or "missing the mark" in Greek).[xxvi] Both of these conditions arise through fear and shame, placed on us by society and propagated by ourselves to ourselves and others.[xxvii] We become scared of doing the wrong thing, and as a result we fixate on our behavior and try to shame others into being like us so we can have the security of knowing we are right. The current debates on sexuality and gender identity can be seen as a modern example of this fear/shaming behavior.

Being in a devotional relationship with Jesus can serve as a break in this negative pattern of self-centering and shaming. Whether it is through direct mystical communion, trying to live up to his example, revering his teachings, or in some other way trying to participate in the Reign of God that he pointed toward, a devotional relationship can be the bedrock of a Christian faith that is freeing, not shame-filled or hostile. Jesus believed and taught that all things are a part of the Reign of God, including us, and taught that the simple act of trying to love God, neighbor, and self was all that was necessary for the religious life.[xxviii] By pursuing a life which loves the self, which loves the other, and which loves the fullness of everything (God) we are drawn away from shame, fear, and selfishness and into deeply committed connectedness. This is one way in which Jesus as Savior can be affirmed by ChristoPagan practitioners.

But what about Jesus as God? If he is the Incarnation, then other forms of addressing divinity are invalid, right? This is a line of logic that has been used to oppress and reject anything not Christian. However, there is a way of understanding Jesus as fully human, and fully divine, and still leave the door open to other manifestations of God/dess in the world. Needless to say, I believe that there are many ways of understanding who Jesus is and was, and for those who believe he was an inspired human (no more and no less), there is no need to reinterpret the Incarnation, since it never happened. I am not belittling this line of thought, I know many who believe this and live lives full of love and grace, and as such I am convinced they are following Jesus' essential teachings.

For many Christians however, there is something about Jesus that is substantially different from other religious teachers. I respect the Buddha and his teachings, but I am devoted to Jesus. What is the difference? For myself, Jesus is an Incarnation of the Living God. This is the dominant view of Christianity, regardless of denomination, and I see no reason to reject that belief, provided it is understood broadly. In this discussion, I owe my Hindu brothers and sisters a great deal of thanks, for it is my study of that large religious tradition (that could be considered the largest Pagan religion on the planet)[xxix] that has shaped my thinking on this. Any errors in discussing *avatara* are, of course, my own.

In Hinduism, Lord Krishna is understood to be fully human: he feels and acts human, he lives and dies as a human; yet at the same time he is totally and fully God, being an Incarnation of Vishnu, the sustaining God of the Hindu pantheon. Practitioners often worship him as a full deity in his own right, feeling that Krishna calls to them more than his fullness as Vishnu does.[xxx] *Avatara* are aspects of the Divine, the Infinite given a form that human beings can understand and devote themselves to becoming like. Using this idea, it is possible to see the parallels between Krishna for a Hindu and Jesus for a Christian, and how this understanding is helpful for both an inclusive Christianity and ChristoPaganism.

Jesus, in this view, is both totally human and fully God. He was born to human parents, lived a human life, and, because of his loving resistance to the status quo of hatred and shame, he was murdered to silence his message. Yet, because he was fully God, his message (and he) continued. Jesus as an *avatara* of God seems to me to explain the One with whom I have a relationship, but it neither excludes the idea that God may have other *avatara* when God so pleases (I am not so arrogant as to tell the Divine what to do), nor does it mean people cannot have a relationship with God without Jesus. I can say that Jesus saves everyone,[xxxi] because Jesus is God. However, not everyone will connect to God through Jesus, and for me that is acceptable, since God is more than the *avatara*. For me, the idea of resurrection is thus both a deeply mystical myth of death-and-life, (such as when the corn God dies to produce the harvest) and a profound truth that love can never be silenced, but will always endure.

Note that I have not delved into facts and figures here, we simply do not know what happened to the physical body of Jesus, nor can we explain the different stories surrounding his life. What I believe Christians and ChristoPagans can emphasize, if they are so inclined, is that they do believe in Jesus' true humanity, true divinity, in his life, death, and resurrection, and in the fact that a relationship with him helps us to connect to God. All of these are "traditional" Christian beliefs, but the way I have interpreted them I hope they have become tools of inclusion, not exclusion. Again, this is not the only way to interpret Jesus, but for me this theology provides a reasoned explanation of my devotional relationship with the One that I know was fully human, but Whom I also experience in mystical connection.

Spirit

So far we have looked at God/dess, especially known in the Trinity, and the person of Jesus. Last, we have the Spirit. Theology of the Holy Spirit has often been used for political reasons, instead of to reflect on personal or corporate experience of the Holy. In the early church, the Holy Spirit was seen as the continuing presence of Christ in the church.[xxxii] As the church grew, there was quickly a tendency for charismatic leaders to claim direct inspiration from the Spirit to support their theology. One of these was Montanus (~150 CE) who was one of the first declared heretics by the Church.[xxxiii] His insistence that the Spirit directly informed him gave him an edge over other church leaders who relied on the emerging tradition of the church for their leadership. As such he was condemned. Montanus is important if only because he is one of the earliest illustrations of the political fighting over the inspiration of the Holy Spirit which continues to this day. A quick Internet search of Christian websites will show a decided split between those who feel that the Spirit interferes directly with people (usually Charismatic churches, but a fair number of independent ones as well) and those who feel that the Spirit inspires the entire church, not just certain people (usually the mainstream denominations and especially Roman Catholicism).

Both sides have pros and cons. On the pro side of the direct-inspiration camp; they can be faster to respond to new things in society and they can serve as a challenge to the establishment. On the negative side, there is no way to "check" direct inspiration, no method for weeding out true Spirit inspired messages from people using the Holy as an excuse to promulgate their desire for control and power. In fact, many of the sick, twisted cults that have arisen are a result of people claiming to have a direct conduit to the Divine. Of course, most saints of every faith have also heard directly from God as well. History seems to be the only indicator of whether a person was sick or a saint (and yes, sometimes they are both), something not helpful for those trying to discern right teaching in the moment.

The benefit to believing that the Spirit works through established faiths is that it provides a way to check whether things are solid or not. If someone or some group is claiming that the Spirit wants you to do something new, you have the tradition and teachings of the faith to verify what they say. The downside of course, is that people in power normally do not want to share, and it is very easy to twist the tradition of the church to support those in power.

Questions about the Holy Spirit for this work include: Does She exist? Does She speak to people today (and if so, how)? Does She deserve a place in a ChristoPagan faith? For me, the answer to all these is yes. While we can conceptualize the Divine as Trinity, we also have to consider the transcendent / immanent process as well. For many Christians, and ChristoPagans, the world is an expression of the Divine, but it is not the entirety of the Divine. However, the Divine is within the world, flowing and moving, shaping and growing. For Christians, this God-with-us presence is usually typified as the Holy Spirit. For ChristoPagans, celebrating the Divine in the world as the Holy Spirit seems to make sense, especially if we typify the Spirit within the Trinity as the Mother God, since She is ever-changing yet ever the same; ever-creating the world around us. This image of the Spirit bridges the gap between Pagan and Christian understandings, and personal experience of the wonders of the world lead to a knowledge that She exists. In other words, when I am struck with awe at the beauty of the world, She is at work within me. When I am overcome by compassion, She is at work within me. When I overcome fear and shame to follow the leading of Christ, She is at work within me.

Does She speak directly to people today? As the ever creating Mother it seems highly likely that She has more to say to people than ever before. We are destroying her children- both the world and each other- at a rapid rate, and further we are using faith as the reason to destroy.

A rational, logical way to evaluate whether a claim is from Spirit or from ego is this: look at the central call of Christianity to Love God and love your neighbor as yourself,[xxxiv] then apply people's so-called revelations to this principle to see if they fit. Calls to hate a group or groups; calls to kill others; calls to deface the natural world for monetary gain, none of these seem to me to love our God/dess within the world nor love our neighbor as ourselves. By the same standard, when people say the Spirit wants us to love more, hate less, live more simply and strive to accept the different; these seem to fit the basic formula of Love God and Love Neighbor.

There are many people that will say this is "proof-texting", that is, selecting a verse from the Bible and ignoring other verses that do not fit your idea. It is true, the Bible contains horrible commands to violence, genocide, and brutal destruction. My question is whether those texts are from God, or if they are simply powerful people using God as the excuse to gain more power. In my belief system, Love God and Love

Neighbor are co-joined commands. Anything that sacrifices people to "honor" God is a lie. Anything that sacrifices reverence for the Universe to benefit people is equally wrong. Whether greedy corporations stripping the Earth or fundamentalist religion killing people who disagree, both are ego and power driven, not Spirit-led endeavors. This, in a nutshell, is my religion. It is hard, as an American I know I consume more than most people around the world. I am committed to living simply, but living that out in my consumer-driven society is difficult, and I acknowledge this. Honoring my Pagan side means learning each year to live closer to nature, more simply, and more aware of how my lifestyle impacts the Earth. Honoring my Christian side means seeking to better the lives of everyone I interact with, seeing in them the beautiful child of God that Jesus sees.

These sides are not exclusive. Pagans love people and Christians care about the Earth. Yet both have emphasized one at times to the exclusion of the other, and I believe a Spirit-filled life seeks balance in both. As a ChristoPagan, I see-saw between the two, seeking to navigate my way in a complex world filled with distractions and ego-centric, consumeristic impulses. Love of God and Neighbor has become the central focus for my devotional life and its practical applications.

In the end, people do have to decide for themselves what they believe. People who have investigated all sides of a debate are generally better able to make a considered, prayerful opinion than those who rely on sources that agree with them, but one of the things that happens when you follow the ever-changing Spirit is that She will often lead you to different places over time. Do not allow yourself to become so fixed on an idea that you cannot be changed by the Spirit. This is especially true for people who are engaging in a new way of communing with the Divine, we need to be alert to the fact that this path may enrich us today, but may need to change over time. We should not be afraid of change as long as it lessens fear and shame and promotes *agape* love, but instead we should see change as the hand of the Spirit, leading us closer and closer to the Divine.

As for the last question, does the Holy Spirit of Christian faith deserve a place in ChristoPagan life and worship? I believe that as the Holy Mother of the Trinity she deserves a greater position of importance than She is often given in modern Christian churches. Many churches present a very lopsided Trinity, where the members are not given equal attention or praise, but rather whatever aspect of Deity seems to support the power of the church is placed in the forefront, with the others far subordinate. I simply do not believe that God acts this way. We humans can be power-hungry and obsessed with the pecking order in our relationships, but I do not believe that the Almighty God needs to do so. In fact, the idea that the Trinity is in complete harmony with each other is a traditional understanding of Christian theology.[xxxv] However, people are incapable of understanding the Infinite and so place the Trinity into roles that mirror human life; rather than trying to restructure human lives to mimic the Trinity.

The Holy Spirit represents the continuing Divine presence in and through the world, in and through the church, in and through each of us. By not having a single form, the Spirit can infuse all things with holiness and life, and by being understood as masculine, feminine, both and neither, the Spirit proves again that God is beyond our narrow human concepts. For those of us who have a desperate need for a feminine divinity to connect to, She provides the mothering face of God; ever changing to meet the needs of Her children, yet She remains steadfast in Her plan for all creation. The Holy Mother Spirit is very compatible with Pagan understandings of the Goddess, yet She is also rooted firmly in Christian theology.[xxxvi]

A final note on the Spirit as Mother God is this: Since the Spirit is by her nature both endlessly creative and yet always the same (and always beyond our full comprehension), it goes to reason that She can be known by many names. For some, She is Spirit, Mother, member of the Holy Trinity. For others She may be Isis, Kali, or simply Mother Nature. For many ChristoPagans, She is Mary, Mother of Jesus.[xxxvii] While traditional Christianity would reject all these as idolatry, ChristoPaganism and its more inclusive understanding of God-Incarnation presented here leave this door open for exploration. If worship and devotion make a person more loving of God and Neighbor, then they worship the God of creation, even if they refuse to name God in ways traditional Christian faith understands.

A small note about gender in the Trinity must be mentioned here. Conceptualizing the Trinity as Father-Mother-Child appears to give credence to the hetero-normative life. I am by no means seeking to say that God is only straight. In fact, Christian teaching is consistent that God is beyond sexuality entirely, and any ways in which we engender God are a product of our finite minds seeking a way to understand the infinite God. If this suggested conception of God does not work for you and your faith, then change it. For example, Butch-Femme-Child God could work, as could a completely asexual understanding of God, or a transgendered God. Whatever we conceive is wrong (or at best only partial), since our conceptions can never come close to the Divine reality. I do believe that God wants us to draw near, and that God in love allows us our mental concepts to help us draw near. Use what concept works, as long as it draws you near to the Holy and fills your life with love and grace.

In summary, ChristoPagans can indeed claim God, the Trinity, and Jesus as the Incarnate Savior without needing to feel guilty about any of it. The Christian umbrella is broad enough to encompass this theology, and the Pagan understanding of the Divine does not have to be in conflict with the God of the Bible or the Trinity when interpreted through a more liberal theology.

The Bible

In addition to Jesus, the Bible is the other item that Christians must take seriously. It is also, perhaps, the more contentious item to deal with, since it is from the Christian Bible that we receive information about Jesus and the early church.

To begin, the documents in question that I am discussing are the Christian Bible consisting of the Hebrew Scriptures and the Christian texts also known as the New Testament. For the purposes of this work, the variations in the Hebrew Scriptures between Jewish, Roman Catholic, Orthodox, and Protestant versions are not critical, and so will not be discussed in detail, although they are well worth your attention.

This section is in no way a replacement for solid biblical study, which is too great a field to be given anything but an overview here. However, some basic information about Bible interpretation is important for ChristoPagans since many people will try to use Bible arguments against your beliefs. Long personal experience has taught me that there are three main ways to handle such a challenge. One is to ignore the person and their arguments. One is to not explain what you believe fully, allowing the other person to fill in what they assume when they ask you questions. For example: If someone says "Do you believe in Jesus?" Then you can just answer yes without going into more detail. The other will then fill in your yes according to their worldview. The third major way of dealing with such questions is to engage in a dialogue where you go back and forth with the other about interpretation methods, shades of meaning, and the like. None of these methods is fully right or fully wrong, each has a time and place where they work best.

The first method, ignoring, needs no explanation. The second method, simple answers, is one that a person needs to consult their conscience on. Sometimes a well-meaning person just wants to be sure that you fit their paradigm of behavior and belief, and a simple answer (as long as it is a truthful one) can make things flow more smoothly. I do not advocate lying, but it is not a lie for me to say "yes, Jesus is my savior" (even though I know I mean it differently than they do), and in some circumstances it is far easier to answer simply than get into a fight with someone determined to 'save' me from my 'sins'.

The third method, engaging dialogue, is usually reserved for those persons who are willing to adapt their paradigm, or at least hear differences before rendering judgment. When engaging in this kind of discourse, the ChristoPagan needs to be well informed if they are going to present a compelling case. There is no need to convince others to join your way of believing, but the inability to fully articulate your religious and spiritual life in ways that connect with others provides a stumbling block to acceptance for a faith path that is already confusing to outsiders.

That said, here are the items to be discussed under the topic of the Bible:

- The "traditional" Christian understanding

The "traditional" Christian understanding of the Bible is actually varied. It ranges from seeing the Bible as a source for faith and life, to the Bible as the Inerrant and Inspired Word of God. For most ChristoPagans, the former (more liberal) understanding of the Bible likely to be more common, as it conveys a sense in which the Bible is the story of people's encounters with God which are, in fact, part of a larger story in which various religious traditions have something to say as well. In this view, one can draw from the Bible what is necessary to sustain a faithful spiritual life, without conflict with other spiritual texts, or with scientific knowledge. This view is most accepting of differences between denominations and religions, and being able to explain how the Bible has informed your faith is the important part of dialogue with those who hold this view. I can say that for me, the heart of Christianity is love of God and neighbor, and as long as I can demonstrate that I am trying to do so and follow in Christ's footsteps, people who hold this more inclusive view will usually be able to accept much of my faith journey, even if they do not understand or agree with all of the details.

However, the Fundamentalist position in which the Bible is the 'inerrant' (completely accurate and correct on all things, not just matters of faith) 'Word of God' (directly transcribed by mortals, but so inspired and holy that it is as though God penned the words) has become the general understanding in much of society, and as such it demands attention. The problems with the "inerrancy argument" are legion, but a few items of interest here are:[xxxviii]

1) Textual matters

2) Translation matters

3) Interpretation matters

First, textual matters. Without being a language expert it is very difficult to understand many of the problems encountered when linguists try to translate the texts of the Bible, but a brief summary is that the Bible was written in different languages (Hebrew and Greek) and that there are many times in which the manuscripts we have are damaged, incomplete, or simply not available. As such, the translators use the oldest, best preserved texts they can and they supplement where necessary. There is no single master text of the Bible, there are hundreds and thousands of fragments that translators piece together to make the English text we call "The Bible". The idea that the Bible is "without error" is simply unsustainable due to the fact that there is not "The Bible" but instead lots of pieces of many books that are carefully put together to make the English text. Also, within these thousands of fragments there is a great deal of human error that has crept into the text. Generally very little of this is of theological concern, the texts agree on Jesus' life, death, and resurrection for example, but there *are* errors.

One example of people having faulty theology because of textual matters is in the name of God. In Hebrew, there are no vowels written down. Thus, YHWH is the way the full name of God is written. Because God's name is so holy, many devout Jews would not say it. Instead, they substituted the word "Adonai" or "Lord". Usually this is printed as 'LORD' in English translations of Hebrew Scriptures. Over time the Hebrew language developed a system of vowel points so people would know how to pronounce the words (because many Jews were not speaking Hebrew at home, but Greek). Again, because devout Jews believed the name of God was holy, they put the vowels for Adonai in the name of God (YHWH). 'YaHoWaH' is sort of what this looked like. Zoom forward to the early days of modern Bible scholarship, and the teams of German theologians working on translating the Bible. In German, W is V and Y is J. Thus YaHoWah became JaHoVaH. Look familiar? Jahovah or Jehovah became the sacred name of God...even though it is NOT in the text at all! Some churches and denominations take this very seriously, insisting that Jehovah is the "true name" for God, even though that word does not exist except as a translating mistake. This is but one example of how translation issues and textual matters inform Biblical criticism and render the idea of inerrancy invalid.

Many of the problems that more liberal Christians, and certainly ChristoPagans, face are not even textual variants, but direct translation matters. Two examples of this are Exodus 22:18 and Galatians 5:20 both of which condemn witchcraft (in the King James Version, Exodus

22:18 is the infamous text "Thou shalt not suffer a witch to live" which was the source of many deaths over time).[xxxix] Galatians 5:20 lists 'witchcraft' as a 'work of the flesh' and thus corrupt.[xl] However, the words translated as 'witch' and 'witchcraft' are emphatically NOT what we would associate with ChristoPaganism. The word in Hebrew is specifically directed at women who cast an evil spell on people.[xli] In no way does it refer to healers, or to modern Pagan practices. The Greek word is related to our modern words pharmacy and pharmaceuticals, and likely refers to the practice of poisoning people. Again, modern Pagan practice does not involve poison, but poor translation choices mean in order to help people past these apparently negative passages one must have a grasp of the original language and what it meant. (Note that passages discussing homosexuality in the New Testament stem from the same problem, although that discussion is beyond the scope of this book).[xlii]

While it would be wonderful to say that translators are holy men and women who receive inspiration from the Divine to offer the most truthful translation, the truth is that translators are people, and people have agendas. Most Bibles are translated by committees, and funded by groups with agendas. As such, things creep into the text that are simply not in the original languages, but which impact so many of our issues in society today. Fights about witchcraft, homosexuality, women's rights, abortion, and other topics are often a result, at least in part, of poor or agenda-guided translations. Even when many of these passages are translated well, the meaning is not finished with translation, as there are still matters of interpretation to consider.

The "traditional" method of interpretation in modern Christianity is the 'literal' one, that is, reading the Bible as though it was absolute historical fact, and further as though it was one seamless book from beginning to end, with no variations of content. This is not only incorrect, it makes a mockery of the Bible leading many to reject it whole cloth as false and wrong. This way of reading the Bible is usually where antimodernity arguments are to be found, such as the 'creationist' movement which treats the Bible as a science text instead of a work of faith. This way of looking at the Bible is actually not the primary one throughout history, but in American life today it is prevalent enough to need to be addressed.[xliii]

The Bible is a collected group of works from over 2,000 years, which contains most literary genres. There is romance (Ruth), fantasy (Jonah), ancient-style biography (Gospels), history (Chronicles), poetry (Psalms), erotica (Song of Songs), philosophy (Job, Ecclesiastes) and so on. Just as you would not pick up a romance novel and expect it to be the literal love story of real people, neither can you pick up the Bible and expect every book to conform to the same standard. Knowing the genre of a given book, or part of a book, is the first step to interpretation.

Interestingly enough, even the 'literal' readers get creative in places. Apparently, the idea that the Bible has graphic sex in it makes these folks nervous, so they claim that Song of Songs is about God's love for Israel. While it is, in fact, a book full of hot graphic sex that is very toned down in English translations. What is wrong with sex? Nothing, according to this book. Yet most people never hear the erotic parts, because traditional translation and interpretation make it "pure". This is an example of translation and interpretation helping to create a problem, in this case Christianity's hostility to sexual expression.

Also, 'literal' readings gloss over the many contradictions in the Bible. There are, for example, two completely different Creation accounts in Genesis that are not even close to being the same. There are two different birth narratives in the Gospels. Wise Men and Shepherds never, ever met, regardless of what children's plays would have you believe. So which story is 'true'?

The idea of truth is another problem the Bible faces. The modern idea that truth only exists in verifiable accounts has caused much trouble in our world, and especially in religion. There are truths that cannot be verified by science or history, but that are true nonetheless. That there is beauty in a sunset, that my family loves me, that life is worth living...these things are all *true*, although none of them are objectively verifiable. The same is what goes on in the Bible. Early people of faith recorded their experiences for their communities in their day, and enough people found the accounts helpful to their faith to keep using them. It took hundreds of years for the canon of the Bible to be complete, and even to this day there are variations on the Bible (number and placement of books especially, but also textual inclusions and rejections in different versions).

One way of looking at these differences is to say the Bible is false, that is, not scientifically verifiable. Another way of looking at this is to see that truth takes many forms, and to be open to interpretations that expand truth. Even history and science, fields usually considered "true", are constantly changing as new facts are discovered, old theories updated and edited, and in both fields the facts must be interpreted to make sense, and the interpretations change over time. The same thing happens with the Bible. New texts are discovered, old translations are updated and scholarship continues to both help and hinder the progress of faith.

A way of interpreting the Bible that sees it as a work in progress, because people are a work in progress, allows us to continually re-read the texts and seek in them new ways of being as a society. For those of us that do not have access to the original texts, a solid translation with a less conservative agenda is important. For myself, I read *The Inclusive Bible* by Priests for Equality. While I doubt that they would understand my spiritual path, their translation of the Bible is solid, welcoming, and clears up a lot of the troubled passages that have caused grief to many people. One of the best things that any Christian or ChristoPagan can do is read lots of different translations, especially those passages that are confusing, or that are interpreted as being against a person or group of people. Commentaries of various outlooks are also helpful for understanding how a given denomination or theological outlook understands the Bible passage in question.

Before continuing to a new topic, one thing that must be discussed is biblical worship. Much of the Bible is very strict against idolatry, that is, the practice of worshiping any God but the God of Israel (known to Christians through Jesus). For ChristoPagans, and anyone seeking to blend two faiths, there is a strong need to weigh their personal experience of the Divine against both traditions and be at peace in their own heart about whatever decisions are made. I do not think the Bible is inherently against calling God by different names, after all, there are many names and titles used for God throughout the Bible.

Perhaps the best guide here is serious study of the Bible, and the ways in which worship is supposed to influence a person's life. Is a given act of worship increasing love of God and of neighbor? If these things are happening, then there is a good chance that the person is on the right track. This is how I make peace between my faith choices, by weighing them against whether or not a given practice makes me a more loving person. Others might give less weight overall to the Bible, or come up with a different theological perspective that enables their syncretism to work. However one does it, for ChristoPagans engagement with the Bible is an important part of their Christian perspectives and it should be an ongoing portion of their spiritual journey.

Leaving Christian discussions aside, for now, we turn to Pagan understandings of the Bible.

- The "traditional" Pagan understanding

The traditional Pagan understanding of the Bible is that it is an inherently hostile document that another religion uses to persecute and murder innocent people. In short, my argument is that the Bible is not antithetical to Paganism, or other faiths, although the ways in which it is translated and interpreted certainly often are. There is no getting around the fact that terrible things have been done in the name of Christianity. However, there are also many, many good things that have been done in the name of Christ, and as such I choose to see the wrong as human failure rather than a fatal flaw of the religion.

The Bible references to witches and witchcraft have been shown above to be due to poor translations, not an objection to the practice of prayer, ritual, healing, and magick that Pagans do. I assume that Pagans will not run around poisoning others, since I assume that no decent person would do so. Thus, the traditional arguments that the Bible is antithetical are groundless and based in human error. The sad truth is that for many centuries in the West, anything not Christian was seen as evil, and many Christian denominations hold this view today, even of other Christian churches which disagree with their own. However, that is not a view demanded by the Bible or by Jesus, it is people interpreting the texts to fit their agendas.

The Bible is used as an argument against blending faiths, and in fact a great deal of the Bible discusses the need to be separate from other religions. However, there are two points to consider here. First is whether a given interpretation is restrictive or permissive, and second is whether a given text is universal or situational. Theology generally sees the Bible in two different ways. Either everything that is not explicitly forbidden is permissible, or everything that is not explicitly allowed is forbidden.[xliv] In other words, a more liberal theology says that unless the Bible forbids an action, it is generally allowable; while a conservative theology says unless the Bible allows an action, it is forbidden. This overall tendency is at the root of much of the modern debate over social changes.

In the context of this discussion, there is also the issue of whether or not a text that might apply is situational or universal. Christians agree that much of the Levitical codes do not apply, but some churches still want to hold people to part of them, believing that while the injunction against eating shrimp or pork is no longer valid, the injunction against same-sex sexuality still applies. This is an example of people considering one passage to be universal (the injunction against same-sex sexual relations) and another passage situational (eating of 'unclean' foods) even when they are in the same part of the Bible.[xlv]

A permissive approach to the Bible that has a strong sense of situational theology is helpful to those blending faith traditions. One example of this is found in Luke 10:25-37. The man asks Jesus what the requirement is for true life (eternal life as it is sometimes translated). Jesus replies that loving God with all one's heart, mind, soul, strength; and loving one's neighbor as oneself is sufficient. A permissive theology like my own uses this as a central text to illustrate that as long as a person is growing in love of God and neighbor, they are spiritually acceptable. Regardless of what other names the person uses for God, or their background, or their practices, so long as the person is growing in love, they are acting according to the code of conduct for the faith. This theological outlook is most welcoming to mixed-faith understandings, so long as the people involved can both agree on the centrality of love.

- The arguments against blending the Christian and Pagan understandings

The argument against blending two faiths is simple. When someone believes that their way is the One True Way, then others must join them or be shunned. This attitude is what is causing the "us vs. them" wars of quasi-religious nature in the world today. Muslims, Christians, Buddhists, Hindus, Jews, and others are fighting each other with both words and weapons in an attempt to convert people to their point of view. In every faith there is a very real human need to be *right*, to have The Truth, to be at the top and secure in their position. Sadly, many people feel that violence is the only way to 'prove' their case and to maintain their hold on followers. This is abusive, and it reduces religion to proof-claims backed with bullets, instead of seeing religion as a means to shape the human heart toward compassion and good.

This fundamentalist view is not only anathema for blended religious life, it is anathema to the goal of world peace, love, tolerance, and inner change espoused by most world religions. What this view does well is serve the desire of people to feel secure. When you are right and others are wrong, you have security of belief if not of practice.[xlvi] However, in a world increasingly devastated by such polarizing thought-processes, even the tenuous security offered by such a world-view is easily shattered by someone else's polarizing thoughts, especially when they are willing to resort to violence to demonstrate their 'superiority'. This book attempts to offer a different world-view which maintains that, although different, various beliefs can provide equal security to believers without the need for it to become a one-way discussion about who is absolutely 'right'.

- Suggested theology for blending Christian and Pagan understandings

Some of the best theology for blending Christianity and Paganism happened in early Celtic Christianity. While today we would look askance at the punishing ways they treated women and their own bodies, these early church monastics also understood the value of nature and saw the entire world as the expression of God's self.[xlvii] Studying this strand of spirituality is difficult due to the Roman Catholic Church's desire to unite all Western Christians under Rome, both in loyalty and in practice, which led to the suppression of Celtic teaching. There are some good books which go into more detail about this early form of Christian practice in the Suggested Reading. The main thing to glean here, for the purposes of ChristoPaganism, is the focus on a holistic form of faith in which there was no split between mind/body/soul, between person/creation, and which held all of life was meant to be holy and sacred; in Celtic Christianity the Divine should be experienced in every activity of life, not just in church.

ChristoPagans have much to offer in the way of new forms of biblical interpretation as well, helping to reclaim the field of bible studies from fundamentalism and bringing new insights and meaning to the texts, both through scholarship and through lived experience. If new interpretations emerge that are focused not on specific actions but on overall growth in love, not on individual proof texts but on understanding the whole of God's love for humanity; perhaps new strands of understanding could emerge that would bring people together instead of polarize them.

Another way of blending theology on this subject is through the deliberate use of symbols. Many Pagan writers have gone into detail about the way the early Christians adopted (some say stole) symbols and ideas, and even gods, from the native religions they encountered. This practice of adapting existing symbols for a new religious purpose is common across religions (for example, the Qaba or Ka'ba, the sacred black stone of Islam, was used as an object of worship for centuries before the Prophet's revelation)[xlviii]. Common symbols adapted into Christianity are symbols of the cycle of life/death/new life that Pagans understood as important for the seasons of nature, while Christians understood them as symbols of Christ's triumph over death. For ChristoPagans, both meanings can hold true. Jesus' resurrection is a powerful symbol of the way in which Love lives beyond death. The symbols used to remind us of this truth can also serve to remind us of the way in which life continues, the security of the fact that the natural order continues, that the Divine is made manifest in every flower, and they can serve to propel the worshiper into deeper spiritual connection with the Holy.

We live through symbols, now more than ever as pictographic representations replace words on signs and globalizing forces seek the common ground between languages. In this time and space, the shaping of symbols into new meanings is common, but instead of being reduced to corporate logos, faithful worshipers can, and should, reclaim symbols for religious purposes in ways that promote faith through diversity, not faith at the expense of diversity. The Bible can be one of these symbols that has meaning in itself and also meaning in pointing beyond itself to the God of love and grace. In reclaiming symbols and creating new meaning for existing symbols, ChristoPagans have a unique opportunity to educate others about this hybrid faith and that celebrate the diversity of our faith, and of life itself.

The Earth

Our relationship to the Earth has always been tumultuous. Early Pagan religions strove to gain the favor of the Gods for their crops and herds, early Christian beliefs varied from closely connected to a sense of distance from the earth, and for many a sense that people were entitled to rule the earth and were not responsible for their actions.

- The "traditional" Christian understanding

The traditional Christian understanding of the Earth comes from Genesis 1:26-28, in which God gives 'dominion' over Earth to the newly created human beings. This 'dominion' was interpreted for many centuries as the ability for people to do whatever they wished, since they were in charge of the planet. This sense of entitlement, coupled with the deep-seated belief that Earth was in fact just a stopping point on the way to Heaven, meant that environmental concerns did not get much attention from individual Christians or from Christian denominations. By the time of the Industrial Revolution in the West, this attitude had pervaded philosophy as well, and many 'rational' people firmly believed that as 'reasoning' beings, humans were entitled to the planet's resources. In the past 25 years, it has become critically apparent, both to denominations and to individuals that the planet is fragile and will not continue to sustain us without changes to our behavior. Today, it is common to find recycling programs at churches, and to have environmental concerns be a topic at denominational meetings across theological preferences.[xlix]

- The "traditional" Pagan understanding

Paganism, in its modern incarnation, has always been at the front of environmental projects. In fact, it has been so strident in caring for the environment that for many years the environmental movement in America was identified with 'New Age' people. Currently, there is a wide diversity within Paganism, with some extremists believing the earth needs to be rid of humanity, while other Pagan groups are not focused on the environment, choosing instead to concentrate their attention on reclaiming ancient religious practices. A quick search of Witches' Voice or other similar sites will reveal the spectrum of Pagan action on this subject.[1] In general, Pagans continue to be very involved with environmental issues since, for many of them, the Earth is a literal manifestation of Goddess, and as such must be honored and worshiped.

- The arguments against blending the Christian and Pagan understandings

A common, if lamentable, argument against blending the two understandings is that any acknowledgment of the Earth as sacred is idolatry and against Christian teachings. From the Pagan side, the argument is that without honoring the Earth as Divine, humans are arrogant and cannot properly care for it. Both of these suffer from the hostility and misunderstandings that have plagued both religions.

- Suggested theology for blending Christian and Pagan understandings

In today's world, taking the earth seriously is both a local and global concern. Pagans have lambasted Christianity for not taking the Earth seriously enough, and far too often they have been right. However, there are serious theologians trying to remedy the neglect and maltreatment of the Earth.[li] Panentheism, as shown above, offers a theological method for understanding God as within the Earth our home while still maintaining the transcendent majesty of the Divine beyond our ability to perceive tangibly. In addition to Creation Spirituality, one other branch of Christian theology that has been especially active in this is Process Theology.[lii] Process Theology is a school of thought which believes that everything and everyone, including God, is in process. God, as a relational entity, is changed by relationship to all of creation, including humanity. God, in this school of thought, is not a static being existing outside of creation and simply letting the world go along; rather God is directly involved with everything that occurs inside creation, always trying to aid the best possible outcome. Free will and the infinite series of action/reaction combinations mean that 'the best possible outcome' does not always happen, but God keeps working, keeps 'luring' or 'wooing' towards what is best.

A side note of importance, Process Theology brings up the idea that God can and does change. If this is the case, then the religious life which seeks God must also change. Thus, ChristoPaganism is not simply the product of people apart from God, but might in fact be the result of people being 'wooed' by God toward a greater sense of good.

While critiques of this theology are many, Process Theology also offers a unique perspective on our relationship with the planet. God is seen as within and beyond the world. Therefore, to have a healthy relationship with the planet is to have a healthy relationship with God, and *vice versa*. This blending of Pagan and Christian traditional understandings is a hallmark of this theology that render it especially useful for ChristoPagan discussions of how we are to understand and care for the Earth.

In this view, the Earth is not simply a thing, it is in fact a part of God. Because of this, the Earth has an intrinsic holiness deserving of honor and respect. While theologians differ in how much reverence the Earth should be given, no Process Theologian discounts the importance of the Earth for religious life. Pagans can resonate with this idea of the Earth as a Divine incarnation, while Christians can see Panentheism as a middle ground between believing the Earth to be a separate Deity (Pantheism) and the Earth being an object totally separate from God (Theism). In today's world, with such a growing focus on the need for humanity to protect our home, the theological idea that the Earth is sacred, a vital part of the Divine, is valuable and important. From a Christian perspective, seeing the Earth as infused with God's presence means that we can take caring for the Earth as a serious act of worship, while still respecting the fact that God is more than just the Earth. In this way, the Earth functions much like the *avatar* idea presented earlier. The Earth is one more revelation of God that takes a concrete, tangible form (incarnation) while still only being a portion of the whole that is God.

Instead of seeing the Earth as holier than humanity, or as lesser than humanity, Panentheism understands that all Creation- from the atom to galaxies- contains the Divine essence within it. God is, in this view, the generative force which holds all that exists together. God is also much more than that. This both-and theology is appealing to a mixed religion like ChristoPaganism since it honors both traditions while forging a middle ground that is distinct from the "traditional" view of either side. We cannot care for people without caring for the planet, and the reverse holds true as well. Instead of favoring one over the other, ChristoPagans are called to walk a middle road wherein they offer a challenge to the status-quo on many issues, including the environment. Some examples include: asking whether world hunger is more a lack of distribution than resources; standing up to those who would engage in poor environmental practices for sheer profit, when for a lesser profit there are better, more sustainable ways to manage the issue; and living simpler lives, leading by example what it means to be in harmony with the planet.

These are, of course, only 'tip of the iceberg' suggestions. Both the human factor and the environmental factor must be taken into account when dealing with a given issue. Issues of social justice, like the need to offer better public transportation so we can eliminate emissions from cars; ensuring the poor have access to inexpensive, nutritious fare; and so forth, also play into this. ChristoPagans can neither stay silent about the planet nor can they ignore the fact that both extremes are fraught with hypocrisy. Environmental leaders using private jets; corporations using substandard materials; the general public electing poor leaders into office over and over again; all of these are things that need to be changed, just as I need to be sure to recycle my cans and plastic. It is a both-and equation that begins with changing our daily attitude.

A note about health goes here as well. We, humans, are important parts of the created world, and important parts of the Divine which is being made manifest throughout Creation. As such, we have a holy duty to treat this God-stuff inside us with appropriate reverence as well.[liii] Physical, mental, social, spiritual, we need to care for our bodies as well as our souls. Thus, exercise and good nutrition, learning to deal with stress, and having healthy social networks and mental stimulation are all as important for the planet as recycling and consuming less. We are a part of the planet, and a part of God, to believe otherwise is to allow disharmony to creep in and rule us. This disharmony, this sense of being alone, separate, or out of tune with the Divine is that part of the human condition that a devotional religion seeks to remedy, not through an hour on Sunday, but by infusing every moment with the awareness of the Sacred, filling each breath with the love of God and Neighbor.

Sin/Salvation/Evil/Good

Sin is often understood as the defining feature of the Christian life. In a Calvinistic view, everyone is totally corrupted by sin and doomed to hell from birth, and only Jesus' sacrifice on the cross can redeem a few souls from this fate.[liv] This gloomy view has been rejected by many, and in Pagan circles a rejection of this view has led to many believing there is no such thing as sin or evil.[lv] Some Christians have, in turn, accused Paganism of being out-of-touch with the world situation today.

Theologically speaking, issues of evil and sin are known as Theodicy. The classic problem of theodicy is *"If God is good, why do bad things happen?"* The answer or answers to this question inform belief systems around the globe. Answers within Christianity typical start with the framework found in Genesis. In essence, people were created good by God, then given the free-will to make choices. We chose badly and as a result, things have been messed up ever since. Within the Jewish tradition the way to rectify this error was to follow the Torah, the Law or Teaching of God given to the people through the Prophets. Within Christianity, the way to rectify this error was to dedicate one's self, physically and spiritually, to following Jesus' teachings. Over time this evolved into the atonement theories discussed earlier in the section on Jesus.

In Paganism, historically, bad things happened because the gods were displeased and so the way to rectify the situation was to propitiate the gods with sacrifices. Sometimes this took the form of an offering at the shrine or temple, from a few grains of rice to a human sacrifice, depending on how bad the situation was. Not all pagan religions practiced human sacrifice, and of those who did, it was usually rare and reserved for the direst situations (like years of drought).[lvi] Another explanation was that bad things like war were really the gods using humanity as their tools. Whichever god won was obviously the most powerful, and thus should be worshiped. This led to much of the combining of gods that happened in the ancient world, when the

Romans conquered Greece, the Greek gods got a makeover (for an overly simplified example).

Modern day Pagans often downplay evil as a whole, in part due to the overemphasis on it by fundamentalism; and in part because the modern form of the religion has been more concerned with the individual or small group's direct connection to the Divine than with making sense of the world. If evil or sin is discussed, it is often in the guise of 'karma', a concept borrowed from Eastern religions. However, using 'karma' as a theological concept implies a world-view that many Pagans would not agree with. As ChristoPagans, some attempt to address the disharmony between both religions on this topic must be made. I do not believe this is a final statement on the topic, the question of evil has been tackled unsuccessfully by far greater minds than my own, but as a starting point, here goes.

- The "traditional" Christian understanding

The 'traditional' Christian understanding has changed throughout the centuries, but the primary pieces of God creating the world good, humans misusing their free will, and Jesus as the one who can save us from our own folly have remained constant. What has changed the most is the idea of sin and evil, and what they mean for the individual person.

Modern fundamentalism likes to define 'sin' as the opposite of 'belief', by which they mean adherence to a specific code of conduct that varies by denomination but always looks like "people different from us". Sinners, according to this definition, are all damned to eternal suffering, and the only hope of avoiding this fate is to adhere to the beliefs and code of conduct of the group. An anonymous quote sums this view up nicely: *"In church I learned that God loved us and that we were all evil and going to hell...and I learned that sex was nasty and dirty and wrong, and should be saved for someone special"*.

This insane God is a common view today, and with this presented as the "Christian" view, it is no wonder so many people reject it. This seems to be a straw man, but in fact the reason many mainline churches are dying is that they reject this presentation of God, yet have not found a compelling theology of their own to explain good and evil. Fundamentalism is very clear about who is "in" and who is "out", so for people needing security this is a compelling way of life. Its primary downfall is not in the clarity of the system, but in the fact that any fundamentalism rejects the billions of people on the planet that do not follow the same "right beliefs", thus requiring people to worship a "loving" God that condemns billions of people for being in the wrong place at the wrong time. There is a "soft" version of this fundamentalism that says if people never hear about Jesus that they are only judged for what they did know, but that people who had a chance to have Jesus and rejected him are damned. Given that these churches are involved in missionary efforts, it seems like they want to offer Jesus so more people can be damned. Within this theology there is a near-dualism which personifies Evil as Satan, the Adversary of God locked in an eternal power struggle. While God will eventually win,

Satan is fighting a good fight, and in fact the only way for God to win may very well be the destruction of all of creation.[lvii] It is an odd theology that I cannot reconcile with the idea of God as unconditional love and as such cannot accept. It is, however, a prevailing understanding of Christian theology today (even if it is not what most Christians believe).

- The "traditional" Pagan understanding

Again, many times Pagans have not dealt with the subject, seeing evil not as institutional or corporate, but as an individual problem. Pagans agree that actions have consequences, and usually (though not always) ascribe to the idea that what you do either a) comes back to you in this life or b) stains your soul as bad karma, forcing multiple reincarnations to burn it off. How the accounting of karma is done is not normally defined, it is assumed to be a law of nature much like gravity.

Unlike the original Eastern religions who developed ideas of reincarnation, Pagans do not generally view this world as illusion or as negative; meaning there is an inherent theological confusion when borrowing the idea of karma. In Hinduism and its associated religions (Jainism, Buddhism, etc) the world is seen as a negative (although compelling) place to be escaped. The point of religion is to purify the mind/soul so as to escape this world and any future reincarnations. Negative actions trap the soul in the cycle of reincarnations, forcing a return to the negative world. If Pagans believe that the world is positive, it seems odd to follow any idea of karma.

Some Pagans have a more Celtic view, that the soul rests between incarnations and that the goal of life is for the soul to learn certain things. Sin is thus failing to learn the right things and committing negative actions. In any view of reincarnation, the goal is for the soul to eventually ascend beyond physical incarnations.

- The arguments against blending the Christian and Pagan understandings

The difference between these views can be stark. Fundamentalism says if you are not like me, you are damned in some way (This is true of every kind of fundamentalism, whether Pagan, Christian,

Muslim or anything else); while a more liberal understanding says that your actions harm your soul, and your connection to the Divine and to other people.

Arguments against are basically from the conservative camps which see no harmony possible between faiths. Whether extreme Pagans who insist that there is no such thing as sin or evil, or extreme Christians who believe if you have not been initiated into their exact type of Christianity you are damned to hell; both extremes make conversation virtually impossible. When dealing with these extremes, the ChristoPagan faces the dilemma of whether or not to initiate a conversation at all, and certainly when confronted by these people it may very well be better to avoid a conversation which will lead to conflict. Sometimes extremists can be talked to and discussed with on a rational level, but often these people have invested their self-worth in the rightness of their group, such that for the group to be flawed would mean they would have to believe they were a bad person. It is a twisted logic that is sad and hard to overcome.

There are perspectives in any religion which will say that if you are not a part of the "in" group, you are wrong/damned/evil/misguided. However, there are perspectives within every religion that are more inclusive as well. ChristoPagans are by necessity members of the more inclusive camp. Through experience, exploration, questioning, and inclination, those seeking to blend religious traditions have already come away from the idea that there is only one way to experience faith. In essence, they are speaking a different language from those for whom there can only be a single path.

- Suggested theology for blending Christian and Pagan understandings

One possibility for blending these understandings starts with going back to the discussion of Jesus. Sin was defined there as *separation from the Divine and the tragedy of failing to live up to our potential (hamartia, or "missing the mark" in Greek).*[lviii] Feelings of separation can be explained in many ways, but in part it comes from the knowledge that we are different from anyone else. Fear (of pain, of abandonment, of not being loved) often forms a protective barrier around these feelings of separation. Shame, which is placed on persons for their failures (whether real or perceived), also perpetuates the separation and loneliness since shame usually includes shunning. Fear and shame are negative emotions, placed on us by society and propagated by ourselves to ourselves and others.[lix] We become scared of doing the wrong thing, and as a result we fixate on our behavior and try to shame others into being like us so we can have the security of knowing we are right; or, because we fear being abandoned by the group, we shame ourselves into behaving as the group wishes, even if it violates who we know we are. This happens to children at home and in school, and it continues into our adult religious lives.

As ChristoPagans, if we believe that Jesus has come as an *avatara* of God, if we believe that the Mother Spirit is always in us and with us, then we can be saved from fear and shame. We no longer need to fear being alone, for God is with us (in fact is inseparable from us). We no longer need to be ashamed, for God will always offer us a chance to make the best out of the situation. Yes, there may be negative consequences for our actions, but in each and every choice God will be with us, 'luring' us to the best possible outcome. We have the free will to indulge our fear and shame, but also the free will to make the right choice. We know it is the right choice if it leads to an increase of love for God, for ourselves, and for others. We know it is the wrong choice if it leads to hate, suffering, fear, or shame. In this theology there is not a hard and fast code to abide by, the spiritual practitioner must spend a lot of time cultivating their conscience and their connection to God if they are to make the best choices in a given situation.

If we believe that a relationship with Jesus saves us from being selfishly centered in ourselves, saves us to a fullness of life wherein we see all things as part of God and if we know that we have a place in the life of God, and if we believe we are saved through devotional relationship with Jesus and through our pursuit of our God-nature, then we can do the best we can in a situation and then trust that God is bigger than we are, and able to use our intentions to promote the best possible outcome given the variables. Forgiveness for ourselves and others comes out of the belief that God is always working to bring out the best in everyone. Trust and love, not fear and shame, are the hallmarks of this kind of life.

But what about evil? This philosophy seems to handle individual actions (sin) but there is a larger category of evil that needs to be discussed. Humanity is able to think and act in groups in ways that are very different from the individual, and societies and cultures have an influence that is disproportionate to the individuals within them. In other words, evil is more than the sum of its parts. For example, American culture favors men over women; families with children over single people; cultural Christianity over any other religion, and so forth.

These are evils beyond the ability of any one person to totally change. An example of this is found in language. In English, maleness is the default when speaking generically about humanity. I can make an attempt to correct that in my own work, but I cannot change the entire English language. The fact that for many people today sexism is still not considered a real issue is a pervasive evil that warps society. It is simply impossible for a person in our society not to be shaped in subtle ways by this cultural phenomenon. Even when a person works very hard individually to overcome sexism, there will always be layers in which sexist problems are not considered.

In addition to somewhat subtle things like sexism in English, more blatant issues include things like access to food and clean water around the world. Whether it is a rebel group, violent dictator, fundamentalist religious fanatics, or others; access to the basic necessities of life remain difficult or impossible for millions of people. Is this symptomatic of a larger evil entity bent on the total destruction of the world, or is it merely lots of individuals laden with negative karma?

ChristoPaganism suggests a third perspective, that corporate evils are neither external nor individual, but that they are the collective results of millions of tiny poor choices that have now created a deep hole from which it is hard to free ourselves. Each time a person lets something negative slide by without comment, they dig the hole a bit deeper. Each time a person joins with others to create a positive change, they fill it in a little bit. Evil, in this view, is made up of the collective failures of the human race to follow God's plan of growth in love.

ChristoPagaism is a syncretic faith, seeking to blend elements of two different religions into a meaningful new way for participants to explore the Divine. One of the outdated notions from ancient Christianity that should be jettisoned is the idea of a god of evil. Satan, as described in the Bible, is part of God's court, not a god in and of himself. Later contact with dualistic religions such as Zoroastrianism put God and Satan on equal footing, endlessly fighting for the souls of humanity. For some, perhaps, this personalized face of evil might be useful, but for my own theology I find that it reduces the need to squarely address all-too-human evil that manifests in each of us through our cultural norms.

No one of us can overcome evil in its entirety; but every action we take either helps or hurts its growth. In this view our individual choices do matter, not necessarily in our lifetime, but in the eternal view of God. Instead of feeling negative about the immensity of evil, we should take solace in the greatness of God. Instead of feeling that our actions cannot change things, we should see that every action counts, both for our personal growth and for the entire planet. This maintains the balance between individual and corporate actions, and gives purpose and meaning to individual actions while still understanding that the individual is only one small part of a universal plan.[lx] By constantly trying to align ourselves with Infinite Love, we each chose with every action to become more of what we are, or less. This process of becoming God-like in Love is known in Christian theology as *theosis* or divinization, and makes far more sense for ChristoPagan theology than an emphasis on personal salvation in some afterlife.

The idea of Original Sin fits in quite neatly here. Instead of the traditional Christian understanding that we are born awful and degenerate (Original Sin was seen by Augustine as transmitted by the sex act itself, making sex dirty as well) ChristoPagans can see that we are all born into a world with a deficit and that we often participate in that deficit without being consciously aware of it. I may know that stealing is wrong and not do it (sin or not sin). However, I am generally unaware of the ways that corporations use terrible labor conditions around the world to make my car tires or toilet paper, meaning I participate in this corporate evil, adding to the deficit in the world every day whether or not I know it. Thus, the idea of Original Sin in ChristoPaganism could be seen as an acknowledgment that we are born into systems which are not perfect, and that we participate in them in ways we do not even realize. Much of the modern talk about "privilege" falls into this category. If I am white, I never experience the pervasive racism that exists throughout every American institution, and I benefit from my skin color even if I personally never act in racist ways. This is original sin at work.

To summarize; sin is any action that detracts from growth in love of God, self, and neighbor; while evil is the collective deficit caused by individual sin over time. Original Sin is just the name given to the fact that we are born into cultures that are not perfect, and thus we participate in corporate evil all the time, even when we do not choose to do so consciously. Evil manifests as actions, and as cultural preferences and warped understandings that emphasize shame and fear over love and grace.

Good is seen as growth in love of God, neighbor, and self, and it is believed that God works always to lure individuals toward good and away from evil. Salvation is both individual and corporate, happening individually for the person who has a close connection to the Holy which enables a life full of love; it occurs corporately as the ongoing process by which societies seek to end the fear and shame paradigm and work together to promote good. Salvation is always an ongoing process, enabled by a loving God who works to empower the best possible outcome in any given situation.

As I said before, this schema is a very incomplete sketch of how ChristoPagans can understand good and evil, sin and forgiveness. These issues are conplex, but a careful working through of the issues can give each ChristoPagan a way to view the world and a sense of how to create deep and meaningful change for ourselves and others, through God's grace.

Heaven/Hell/Afterlife

The interesting thing about this section is that it is purely speculative. While near-death experiences have received a great deal of media attention, the simple truth is nobody can prove what happens after death. Early peoples believed in some sort of afterlife, but the details ranged from the shadowy realm of Sheol in Jewish faith to the elaborate afterlife of the Egyptians and Chinese. In Jesus' day there was a great deal of adoption from Zoroastrianism regarding the conflict between good and evil, and the afterlife; with early Christian beliefs ranging from reincarnation to bodily ascension to heaven to nothing much at all.[lxi] Even today, there are large differences between Catholic, Orthodox and Protestants on this subject, with further subdivisions among Protestants.

- The "traditional" Christian understanding

The main understanding of Christianity is that if you are Christian when you die you go to heaven, and if you are not when you die you go to hell. Heaven is a wonderful place where you commune with God; hell is a place of eternal torment for the damned, ruled by Satan. Having said that, this amalgamated understanding of the

Christian afterlife does very little justice to the complexity of belief on the subject. Catholics believe in additional realm(s) for the purification of the soul; Mormons believe that souls may be baptized (and get into heaven) after death; most Mainline Protestants hold that as long as you are a good person you will go to heaven. Each and every denomination has a nuanced and varied view on the subject, with the amount of detail given based generally on how much that branch of Christianity believes that salvation is about going to heaven (as opposed to about a better life on earth). A given clergy person or denomination may give more or less attention to the matter in their churches. Historically, arguments about the afterlife were central to many of the schisms and splits of the church, and while today these differences may remain they have taken a distant back seat to this-life arguments over gender, procreation, and sexuality.

- The "traditional" Pagan understanding

There is no one Pagan understanding, though most non-Reconstructionist faiths lean toward some kind of reincarnation. How often the soul incarnates, and the reasons for incarnating do vary, but Pagans are much more focused on life in this world than the next. The exception to this present-world focus is when Pagans contact and work with what they believe to be their dead ancestors or spirit guides. Since there is no one understanding, beliefs on this subject are all over the map, and it is not considered a central doctrine of the faith, although each tradition may focus on it more or less.

- The arguments against blending the Christian and Pagan understandings

Many Christians believe that reincarnation is incompatible with Christianity. Many Pagans believe that heaven and hell are incompatible with Paganism. The breadth and diversity of opinion on the topic is generally not addressed in either Christian or Pagan discussions on the topic, but that is caused, in part, by the fact that there are so many beliefs and because for most believers of both faiths it is not a core focus in the West, social issues having taken on a much greater presence.

- Suggested theology for blending Christian and Pagan understandings

Some early Christians believed in reincarnation.[lxii] Some Pagans believe in a paradise realm.[lxiii] The fact that the afterlife is neither critical for salvation, nor a primary focus of the modern world (where we can expect to live into our 70's in America) implies that this is an area on which there is room for disagreement. The working paradigm that salvation is from fear and shame to relationship with God does not discuss the particulars of life after death, and I frankly have no clue. I do believe that God is infinite love and that as such, whatever part of me is unique and "me" will still exist in some form or fashion, even if it is just as memories my loved ones (including God) hold.

Angels and demons, to me, fall into the category of Mystery right along with life after death. Many, many people have had visions of Heaven and Hell, of angels and of saints. Many people from all walks of life have had experiences that a purely skeptical perspective cannot explain, except as hallucinations or make-believe. Rather than try to 'prove' or 'disprove' these claims, I suggest looking at them from the same kind of perspective I discuss in the section on divination. Be aware there are many charlatans who will use anything to get money, power and fame. If you never experience such things, you are neither bad nor lacking in faith, and shaming people because they do or don't perceive things differently is not helping anyone grow in love. Having said that, if working with angels, saints, dreams or visions makes you a more loving and compassionate person, then I say go for it.

To conclude this section, I personally treat questions about the afterlife and non-material entities with a great deal of hesitation, trying to keep focused on what I can claim as my experience with more certainty. In the case of life-after-death, the Bible is very clear that God loves all and is bigger than death, and for me that is enough. For a person desiring more, a book of note on this subject, which outlines a Christian

Universalism that I find quite compelling: *If Grace is True* by Philip Gulley and James Mulholland.

Astrology/Divination

This section deals with the theology surrounding human attempts to perceive the future and act accordingly. Special attention is paid to the psychological implications of such practices, and how such practices are or are not helpful for my understanding of ChristoPaganism.

- The "traditional" Christian understanding

The traditional Christian understanding of divination and astrology is that it is evil, and associated with foreign gods and the Devil.[lxiv] The modern view is that it is either of the Devil, or that it is con artists trying to scam people for money; either way it is not helpful for Christian life. However, there are recorded accounts of divination in the Bible,[lxv] and there are incidents where notable theologians in history have turned to divination to make decisions.[lxvi] As such, it seems to have a mixed history, but it is generally seen as silly at best, negative at worst.

- The "traditional" Pagan understanding

The traditional Pagan understanding in ancient history stemmed from the idea that all things were controlled by the heavens. 'As above, so below' sums up the idea that what was going on in the realm above had an impact on the world we live in. Additionally, the idea of ancestors remaining in the spirit realms to protect and guide their descendants was strong in the ancient world; and the blending of these two ideas created most of the divination systems used today. Regardless of the means, divination is seen as a way to anticipate the future and either embrace or change it. In the vast majority of understandings, divination is not set, but is a "most likely outcome" scenario which the person can influence in a variety of ways. Of course, Pagans will admit the number of charlatans which exist as well, but they generally do believe that there are persons who can accurately predict events through various divination methods.

- The arguments against blending the Christian and Pagan understandings

Setting aside any discussion about charlatans, the arguments against blending the two understandings differs depending on whether you have a more Calvinistic or Armenian world-view.[lxvii] In a Calvinistic world-view, everything has been predetermined and as such, divination is useless since things cannot be changed. A person needs to have faith in God and accept whatever happens. This worldview is very prevalent in many Christian denominations (although it exists in other religions as well) and when encountered it is very resistant to discussion, since even the discussion is predestined.

In an Armenian or free will centered theology, human beings are able to make choices and decisions against the desire of God. As such, divination can be seen as 'cheating', since a person is trying to see the outcome to a situation rather than follow their faith and trust God for the results.

In both world-views, there is also a sense in which divination is temptation, since people are relying on other means besides God for inspiration and authority. Most modern theology simply thinks that divination of all kinds is silly, harmless at best and potentially crippling at worst, since rather than relying on their own ability to choose, a person relies on the divination to determine what to do. There are still some groups that would argue it is the work of the devil, tempting people away from God's word, but most Mainline Protestants would simply see it as silly and maybe a way for charlatans to prey on the weak.

Paganism usually holds to a larger world-view than modern Christianity, with the idea being that there are realms of existence beyond what science can prove and describe. Many Pagans believe that things like spirit guides, totems, and divination fall into these realms. Neither side sees belief in such things as a core theological stance; acceptance and use, or disapproval of and non-use do not seem to be a core measure of faith in either religion. As such, there is no need to engage in divination if it is not helpful for the growth in love of the individuals involved; and in fact there is much to be said against it, for many persons struggle with decisions and wish to allow another to tell them what to do. This is dangerous in anything, but especially in religion. One only need look at the wide variety of cults to see the lasting harm inflicted on people who did not critically think through what their leaders and advisers told them. However, for some, divination is a way of making sense of the world that aids in their spiritual growth, and as such, a suggested theology is listed below.

- Suggested theology for blending Christian and Pagan understandings

Modern psychology offers a way to blend these understandings without debating the correctness of any given world-view or stance on predestined actions. In short, some branches of psychology would say that the symbols someone finds important, and the meaning people give to a divination reading, can tell us a lot about who that person is and what they are dealing with in their life. It should be obvious, but just to be sure it is said, if there is any chance that anyone has any psychological issues, they should consult a professional mental health expert who is regulated by the laws of their state. In fact, regular counseling is just a darn good idea for everyone, as it gives you a trained, more neutral perspective on life events.

Divination can never be a replacement for therapy, but for many otherwise mentally healthy people, divination can be a way of meditating, using symbols to allow your subconscious mind to communicate. Speaking not as a mental health professional but as a theologian, I can say this approach seems to balance the desire we have for information about the future with the need to look inside ourselves for answers to our lives. A caution here, few people can be trusted to tell you about yourself, and until psychics or other divination people are regulated, I cannot recommend their use except as a possibly fun and somewhat expensive diversion. Anyone who believes they have truly found a guru, oracle, guide, or so on should ask family and friends about this person, and be willing to listen to what they tell you. Yes, the world is a big place and science does not have all the answers. However, there are many people who will sound religious and fleece the unwary for every dime they can. So be careful![lxviii]

Using things like Tarot cards, pendulums, or other divination methods to explore one's own psyche is a way to explore what your mind is trying to tell you. Dream work, journals, and so on all have their place in exploring what is going on in your head. Consistency is important here, as mental symbols are not standardized, but unique to the person and you have to figure out what your brain's code is. If this method of working is helpful to you, consulting a professional psychological person who specializes in this can be of great value.

Astrology deserves a note in this section as well, mainly to say that it has never been proven accurate for people's lives.[lxix] Some people want to believe that there is a reason and purpose for everything that happens in their lives. Whether because of predestination or because of the alignment of the planets is a personal belief, but the idea that something is controlling your life and compelling behavior remains consistent in that kind of worldview. This framework seems incompatible with the Process Theology idea that God allows free will and is always luring (not commanding) toward the good. This is not to say that the symbolism of astrology is all bad, nor is it to say that a person cannot be a good ChristoPagan if they believe in astrology; what it is saying is that astrology is neither central to the faith, nor scientifically valid, nor theologically consistent with the Universalism and Process Theology ideas that comprise this work. If someone was to take astrological readings and evaluate them for the symbols that resonate with their lives, much as described above with Tarot and dream work, then maybe that could have use for someone's growth in love. For myself, I have not experienced it as useful or beneficial. As always, take that statement, examine in it light of your life and beliefs, and then do as you will so long as it leads to an increase in love of God, self, and neighbor.

Sacraments/Rituals

Sacraments, usually understood as a tangible sign of God's grace, have historically been a mark of inclusion into the Christian faith. In ancient Christianity, initiates (called *Catchumens*) had to study for a period of time before being baptized or celebrating Eucharist (also called Holy Communion).[lxx] Today, only the Catholic and Orthodox churches typically maintain this requirement, although certain churches require a level of understanding and/or a profession of faith before sacraments can be given.

What a sacrament is, and what exactly it does, differ from church to church. In the "high" or ritual-centered churches,[lxxi] sacraments are usually seen as sacred rites, validly performed only by certain persons, which uniquely convey

God's power to the individual. In these traditions, the ritual of the sacrament takes on a magick nature; and the theology of these practices becomes incredibly detailed and convoluted. For the "low" or preaching based traditions, these rites are sometimes seen as sacred (magickal) events, and sometimes simply as observances, that is, things the faithful do because God told them too, but that are without any specific power of their own.

Using the word 'magick' is touchy, because no Christian theology would use that word, but from a Pagan perspective what happens in these rituals is magick, that is, the specific correspondences between words, actions, and symbols which, when combined with the intention of the people involved, leads to extraordinary results. This is important to note for ChristoPagans since the nature and purpose of magick is often a sticking point between religions.

- The "traditional" Christian understanding

The traditional Christian understanding of a sacrament is different between the high and low churches.[lxxii] High church theology says that the sacrament is a ritual which, when performed correctly, will directly impart God's power or grace to the believer according to which sacrament it is. In the case of Baptism, Original Sin is washed away and any personal sins committed are forgiven. In the case of Eucharist, the actual Body and Blood of Christ are consumed (although exactly how that happens differs among churches). In the high churches, there can be as many as seven sacraments, each with a different ritual and effect. The seven are (in order of general occurrence): *Baptism, Confirmation* (joining the church as an adult, also seen as the church giving the person the Holy Spirit), *Eucharist* (also called Holy Communion), Penance/*Confession* (to and with a priest, acting in the place of God), *Holy Orders* (ordination or religious orders), *Marriage*, and Last Rites/*Extreme Unction* (forgiveness of sins at death so soul goes straight to heaven). While God

118

can and does manifest grace in other ways, these are guaranteed by the church to 'work', that is, to convey the power/grace provided the ritual is performed properly.

There was a great controversy in the early church called Donatism[lxxiii] in which a church bishop, Donatus, believed that if a priest was sinful the sacrament was not valid. Since at the time it was believed if one died without baptism one was damned, it is easy to see how this quickly became a big deal. The official position of the church has been since that time that the sacrament is valid if performed correctly, even if the priest is not worthy. However, there are convolutions in all the high churches about this very subject, and the matter is far more complicated than this introduction will allow. Suffice it to say that while the high churches officially say baptism is valid because God says so, it is very likely that a convert to a high church would have to be re-baptized to be sure the sacrament was done right. Additionally, a person ordained according to the proper ritual can still be decreed invalid, even if the ritual followed all proper procedure. This is important for women seeking ordination in the Catholic and Orthodox traditions, church theology says the ritual is valid because it was performed correctly; but also that it is not valid because it was a woman receiving it.[lxxiv]

Low churches have a vastly different view, sacraments are normally limited to Baptism and Communion, and how they are viewed ranges from virtually identical to the Catholic view (removal of sin, Body and Blood of Christ) to simply public rituals that are done because Jesus did them, but that have no merit in and of themselves besides helping people follow Jesus. While these churches historically had lots of theology surrounding their beliefs on the subject, for most Mainline Protestants they are simply things you do at church because Jesus did them; very few teach the theology to the average lay person.

Baptism is more of a sticking point than Communion, many low churches have one valid form of Baptism (usually immersion) and so a person joining these churches might need to be re-baptized to be sure it was done correctly. Again, the exact theology of these churches ranges widely, but the general trend is that they are not magick rituals but rather observances done because Jesus did them. However, individual denominations may very well have more detailed theology depending on their heritage, and usually that can be found somewhere on the denomination's website.

In summary, there are two major trends in Christianity: High churches tend to see sacraments as rituals which, when performed correctly by the right people, guarantee the recipient a portion of God's power/grace in accordance with the ritual; low churches tend to see sacraments as rituals which were instituted by Jesus and thus are observed by the faithful, although they may or may not be guaranteed conduits of grace (depending on the individual church's theology). Since every denomination has shades of meaning and theology around each practice, the only way to know for sure what a given church believes is to check with the church individually. Even then, the official understanding may or may not be what the ordinary member believes happens.

- The "traditional" Pagan understanding

Within Paganism there are holidays, and rituals, but very little in the way of explicit sacraments. As a developing faith, there are emerging initiation rites, coming-of-age rites, and so forth; but there is not the body of work that Christianity has on the subject. Modern Paganism has not had the length of time to develop the depth of theology that Christianity has, although in its relatively short history it has spawned lots of denominations as well. In general the same sort of High/Low split applies within Wicca certainly, and other Pagans to some degree. High traditions have detailed rituals, valid practitioners, and 'guaranteed' results. Low traditions are more focused on what 'feels right' than a formula, and have more fluid experiences of sacred presence.

These are generalities, in every branch of both faiths there is a strong sense that the Holy can and does manifest in myriad ways. In Wicca, and some other kinds of Paganism, the difference between high and low branches is one of detail. In the high traditions of Wicca (and others) there are precise correspondences, pantheons, and ways to perform a rite. In the low branches, things are more flexible. For some traditions, there must be a certain number of people, a gender balance, etc. while in others there is more of a cafeteria feel. Both of these have merit, and each person should explore which style of worship and ritual best connect them to the Holy.

- The arguments against blending the Christian and Pagan understandings

The arguments against blending the two are rooted in God identity, and an understanding of how grace works. In Christianity, grace/ God's power is an external thing, conveyed to the believer through divine desire, and the fact that the rituals of sacraments work is only because God desires it to be so. In Paganism, humanity is endowed by the Divine with power, and can tap into that power to change their reality. A Pagan may petition the gods for aid and receive it, according to divine desire, but a Pagan also has within them an energetic 'battery' that can be used to fuel positive changes. In Christianity, God is wholly Other; in Paganism magick is both Other and Indwelling. Further, there is the simple fact that the names used for God are usually different between the two faiths. Many Christians would say that only through their church can come salvation; many Pagans would say only outside the church can their gods be known.

- Suggested theology for blending Christian and Pagan understandings

ChristoPagan worship and ritual can make solid use of a variety of theological understandings to blend the two faiths. Perhaps the easiest blend is that of the low traditions, precisely because the sacraments are seen as observances, and so there is no mandate to perform them a certain way to guarantee the result. However, for many people, rituals and sacraments are indeed powerful ways by which God connects directly with the believer, and as such I will attempt to weave a way through the high theology of the two faiths to create something both unique to ChristoPaganism, but that also gives honor to the theologies from which it comes.

First, a discussion of what is truly incompatible. There is no way that I can see to validly follow high church and high tradition theology to the letter. For example, a Catholic priest would not perform Mass for a group of Gardnerians, nor would a Gardnerian High Priestess Draw Down the Moon in front of the Catholic priest, at least not in my experience. Having said that, there is a way to create a new tradition of ritual-centered worship which adheres to the high church tradition while forging a new way of understanding the sacramental nature of life.

For this, a beginning discussion of God-identity. Earlier great attention was given to the idea that God lures or woos us to the best possible outcome in any given situation. In this Process Theology type of world-view, each and every action is a separate encounter with God that is infused with the presence of God. Because God is in and through all things, as well as being distinct and separate from all things; both the traditional Christian view that God acts from outside us and the Pagan view that God has given us inner power can be true.

God has, in love, provided us with the inner reserves we need to make the best choice in a situation. Where our reserves run low, God continues to provide us the ability through the Spirit of life that is all times and all places. Rituals, in this view, are both a choice to do what is best and a way to 'refill the tank' within our souls. By setting aside specific times, places, and patterns to connect to the Holy we are making a deliberate choice to seek God, a God who is never apart from us. Thus we look within for the connection to God that has always been there, even though we sometimes forget about it.

Rituals can provide the structure and sacred space within which we can reconnect to the Divine source of life. The more specific the ritual is, the less clutter our minds have to contend with. When we know the patterns of the ritual in our core, we are freed to focus on the encounter with the Holy (instead of wondering what happens next). This is the primary reason for having structure and repetition in ritual. God can, will, and does encounter us in the mundane and the unstructured, but when we deliberately make space for the encounter, it is much more likely to renew us.

An example of this comes from very human romance. Sometimes deeply meaningful romantic encounters happen spontaneously. Those are wonderful and amazing and delightful. However, relying on those alone to maintain the relationship is not a good idea. We need planned times and places without interruption to renew our connection to our earthly loves. In much the same way we need planned times and spaces to encounter God. Over time, the individual or group doing the same rituals enters a meditative state in which repeated encounters with the Holy become the norm, not the exception. This is partially the preparation of the individual, and partially the grace of God. Monastic people from around the world use repetitive rituals involving movement, words, mental images, and symbolic objects to create the 'sacred space' for a holy encounter to occur. For ChristoPagans, this space is created by regular observance of the wheel of the year, as well as additional rituals whenever possible or necessary.

For some worshipers, it is the entire ritual which creates the necessary conditions for a divine encounter. For others, it is a standard part of the service, like Holy Communion. Either way, Sacraments are specifically the tangible things which, when done in a ritual way, convey grace (power of the divine/sense of the divine's presence) to us. ChristoPagans have a deep sense of God's working in and through each individual believer. While there may be 'clergy', that is, people who are set aside to preside over the rituals, and whose advice is theologically informed and trusted on matters of faith; it is also a hallmark of the faith that the rituals can and should be egalitarian, with everyone allowed to participate and lead in turn. The priest/ess is not holier or better than the congregation, and anyone may be a presider for rituals provided they have prepared themselves to do so. With this in mind, and remembering that different groups may choose what meets the needs of their gathering, one possible list of ChristoPagan Sacraments, and the reasoning for each, is as follows:

Primary Sacraments

These are called Primary precisely because they are observed by the vast majority of Christian and Christian inspired religions around the globe. From earliest disciples to the modern plethora of denominations, these two are considered the core of Christian sacraments. As such, it seems fitting that they be included in the practice of ChristoPagans.

Baptism

In the ancient world, baptism was a symbolic cleansing that washed away the old and allowed the worshiper to enter the new world of the faith. For ChristoPagans, this can be either infant baptism, in which the family acknowledges their child as a gift, and in doing so pledges to raise them in the faith; or it can be an adult baptism which symbolically cleanses the old ways of thinking and being, and welcomes the person into the faith. Since sin and salvation are ongoing effects, there is no need to be 'cleansed from Original Sin', but there is a need to take a public stand for the faith, and to participate in a washing away of old mental and emotional constructs. This ritual was practiced by ancient mystery cults as well as Judaism and Christianity; making it very suitable for a Mystery based faith such as this.

Eucharist/ Holy Communion

From earliest times, eating meals together was a sign of solidarity and hospitality. For Christians, the ritual of Communion was instituted by Jesus as a re-telling of the Passover story, and celebrating it was a way to demonstrate their connection to one another and Christ's sacrifice.

There are various ways to understand and celebrate Communion, but the ritual meal and its meaningful Words of Institution are central to virtually all Christian practice around the world; and as such it is important for this blended faith as well. For many Christian groups, the first time a person takes Communion is an especially intense ritual act. Many Christian groups disagree about when is appropriate for children to begin taking Communion, primarily based on whether they see Communion as something for only the faithful to do; or whether they see Communion as a way Christ reaches out to humanity. Theologically speaking, for ChristoPagans it seems more reasonable to include children as much as possible in faith practices from the beginning (so that they do not feel excluded or slighted by faith), and then when they are ready (and understand more of the meaning of what is going on) allow them to lead the ceremony as a full participant.

Secondary Sacraments

These are called secondary not because they are any less valid a means for giving and receiving Divine grace, but because their practice has not been consistent around the globe. In fact, at least one of these (prayer beads/ Rosary prayers) has never been considered an official sacrament of the Christian church. However, any or all of these can be deeply meaningful, tangible ways of encountering the Divine, and as such they are included here.

Anointing with Oil/ Healing Work

From ancient times, it was believed that anointing a sick person with oil and praying for them could bring divine healing.[lxxv] This belief carried over into Christianity, with early church documents giving instruction for this vital healing work. Modern Paganism, with its focus on magickal workings, including healing, makes this ancient sacrament very fitting for a blended faith practice.

Confirmation/ Coming-of-age

When infant Baptism is practiced, the family is promising to raise the child in the faith. For those traditions, a coming-of-age ceremony is important because it is when the child declares for themselves the desire to follow the faith, often demonstrating knowledge of the faith by writing a statement, leading part of a service, etc. When infant Baptism is not practiced, the coming-of-age is usually when the Baptism is held, since the participant is declaring allegiance to the faith.

Whether or not it includes Baptism, a coming-of-age ritual is very meaningful as it signifies when the child is considered responsible for their own moral decisions. From that point on, religiously speaking, the child cannot blame the parents, the child must accept the consequences of their own actions before God. In modern America, where this coming-of-age ceremony has dwindled away, there is a great deal of meaning and value to be gained by promoting an initiation into adulthood.

Marriage

Loving relationships are understood as a gift from God, and as such, the presence of the other can be a tangible means of receiving God's grace. Seeing marriage as a holy act, as a covenant between the partners and God, can make marriage a place to encounter the holy. Under no circumstances should fear or shame be a part of this process, either in the making or in the dissolving if that ever happens. Instead, people should be helped and aided in the formation of solid, loving relationships based on mutual commitment and aligned life-goals; and the idea of marriage as a Sacrament is meant to aid that process; not to imply that if the people involved fall short that they are bad or sinful. Also, care should be taken not to force single people into marriage if that is not their calling in life. Finally, marriages have a theology of their own, which should never be limited to 'man and woman having children'. That is but one of the myriad ways that human beings can choose to live in God-filled covenant with each other and the world.

So long as a relationship is promoting the growth in love of God, self, and neighbor that ChristoPaganism values so highly, it is a good relationship and should be celebrated as such. If people wish to make a formal declaration of their relationship in a certain way (i.e. marriage), the church should support them with rituals and theology that are expansive, inclusive, and that embrace the loving care that God has for us and that we are to share with one another. Limiting the gender or number of adults in loving relationship, or tying the relationship solely to childbearing, makes a mockery of the idea that love is ever expanding and growing.

For those who wish to live as partners together in a covenant built around faith and love, creating a home life together and sharing in all that happens to each other in the course of their lives; the church should celebrate their covenant with appropriate rituals and Sacraments of marriage.

Marriage, in ChristoPaganism, is the public ritual during which the church celebrates the intimate connection of persons for the purpose of living their lives together, publicly and privately, as a family; with the church witnessing a mutual declaration of

support, companionship, and sharing which empowers all involved to connect to God, self, and neighbor more openly and lovingly.

Prayer beads/ Rosary

Many Christians and Pagans alike hold to a tradition of using a beaded cord or chain during prayers. This physical symbol helps with the mundane aspects of counting prayers, gives tactile stimulation during prayer time, and connects the worshiper to all those who are engaging in the same prayers around the world.

Almost every religion uses prayer beads in some way, and for many ChristoPagans the Rosary in particular has significance, since the Scriptures and prayers used are traditional to Christianity, but the focus is on Mary; whom, as we have already seen, may act for believers as an *avatara* of the feminine face of God. The prayers of the Rosary are traditional, but they can have some theological difficulties for ChristoPagans. As such, there is an appendix at the end of this work with alternative Rosary prayers that I myself use in devotions.

Non-sacraments

Holy Orders, Confession/Reconciliation, Chrismation. These are not considered to be Sacraments by this work, and here is a brief explanation of why for each one:

Holy Orders refers to the fact that in the high churches, ordination is considered a sacrament. The egalitarian nature of ChristoPaganism seems to be at odds with the idea that there could be a means of Divine grace that is only available to the few. As such, Holy Orders are not considered a sacrament for this work. Further, there are a lot of legal issues around calling oneself clergy, and as such they are beyond the scope of this work.

For persons seeking legal recognition of their status, consult with local laws for the process. This book is not a legal work, and does not offer any advice about legal matters. For ChristoPagan rituals, a sense of egalitarianism should prevail, in keeping with the openness of the faith. Thus, anyone who is prepared may lead a ritual, it does not need to be an ordained clergy for the ritual to connect participants with the Sacred.

Confession/Reconciliation. Paganism is centered in the idea that there is no mediator between a person and God. Christianity is centered in the idea that the only mediator needed was Jesus. Thus, neither religion inherently feels that individuals require another human being to help them connect to the divine. Finally, there are legal implications to what kinds of confidences can be kept in by religious leaders, and again legal matters are beyond the scope of this book. There are times where this rite can be very meaningful for all involved, since sometimes it is important to look another person in the eye and hear aloud that one is forgiven and loved by God, but it is not considered a Sacrament for this work.

Chrismation. In Orthodox Christianity, this is the ritual by which a baby is anointed with oil and given by the church the gift of the Holy Spirit.

ChristoPaganism does not believe that the Spirit is controlled by the church, rather we believe that, while She empowers the church to make loving decisions in line with the faith, She is in fact beyond any form of capture, being the male/female, tangible/intangible, active/passive and just all around hard to define part of God.

The above list is by no means a complete list, groups may add or subtract Sacraments as needed for the religious life of the group. One thing to consider when doing this, however, is the theological implications of each act. The above list was compiled from the historical sacraments of the Christian faith, many of which have roots in Pagan counterparts of antiquity. These tangible signs of God's grace have proven themselves throughout the centuries, and for a group to refuse to embrace at least Baptism and Communion means that they are distancing themselves from much of Christianity.

In a faith that is already considered 'different' at best, and 'heretical' at worst by the rest of Christianity, some may see it as necessary to stick as closely to the practices of Christianity as possible. Others, rejecting the idea that following Christ is limited to the rituals of the historic church, may refuse to do any of these things. Most likely, the majority of groups will arrive somewhere in the middle, adopting some practices and rejecting others, based on their interpretation of the Bible and their personal experiences with God. This is acceptable provided those involved can both articulate why they are doing what they are doing and be accepting of others who do it differently.

ChristoPaganism is about doing things in a new way, and we must be humble about what we do, lest we make the same mistakes our forebears have; thinking we have the One True Way and belittling all others. Let us live lives full of love and grace, celebrating the wonder of the Holy Presence, and always let us remember that God is Mystery, beyond our understanding and closer than our next breath. May each Sacramental celebration draw you nearer and nearer to this amazing and awesome God. *Amen and Blessed Be.*

Magic/Prayer/Meditation/Energy

This section encompasses a variety of actions, all of which involve the ritual use of our bodies for internal or external purposes. The primary difference between Paganism and Christianity in some of these actions has been a debate about the source of the energy used- whether it is 'external' or 'from God' or 'internal power' from within. ChristoPaganism, as presented here, sees this as a false dichotomy, since God acts in and through all things, including human beings. As such, these terms are not necessarily as distinct as some groups would make them out to be. In the 'traditional' sections they are treated as separate, but in the blending section they are treated more interchangeably.

- The "traditional" Christian understanding

The traditional Christian understanding of magic is that it is evil (perhaps because of its association with old religions, perhaps because it took power to heal away from the auspices of the church, either way the tradition is that magic is negative). Prayer, seen as communication with the Divine, is acceptable and encouraged behavior, and takes many forms. Various Christian writings throughout history discuss the methods and means of prayer; but in general prayer is understood as one or more of the following:

→ **Adoration**: prayers praising and adoring God for being God

→ **Thanksgiving**: prayers thanking God for specific events

→ **Intercession**: prayers to God on behalf of someone else

→ **Supplication:** prayers for yourself

→ **Contrition**: prayers to God asking for forgiveness.

Many writers link these kinds of prayer to the ways God is addressed in the Bible, but these types of prayer also cover virtually every human situation and so are fairly uniform in that respect.[lxxvi] Prayer is sometimes with words, sometimes with actions; but most important is the intention. In fact, the intention (desire of the person) is considered the most important aspect of prayer.[lxxvii]

In certain Christian traditions, angels or saints may also be objects of prayer, not as gods in their own right, but as intercessors who will pray to God on your behalf.[lxxviii] Many Christians believe that the more people you have praying, the higher the likelihood of a positive outcome; and for some, the more illustrious the person, the higher the likelihood. Thus, having a bishop or the Pope or the Blessed Mother herself praying for you gives you a 'leg up' on your request. Some theologians decry this, since God is not to be manipulated by our whims. In fact, the best form of intercessory prayer is perhaps non-directive, that is, instead of asking for a specific outcome, the intercessor simply asks for God's will to be done in a situation. This runs the risk of fatalism; instead of seeing that God's will is for the good, people can blindly accept whatever happens as 'God's will'. The benefit, however, is that our wants are disconnected from the larger sense of God's plan for the entirety of creation. If I did not get that bike for Christmas, God is neither mean nor non-existent, it was just not the plan at the time. Both sides of this argument have merit, and both have flaws, especially with regard to healing prayers.[lxxix]

Fatalism, or predestination, says that there is no change possible, one may only learn to accept what happens. This is helpful when it means people quit beating themselves up about what they cannot control; but it is unhelpful when it means people do not change situations and systems they can influence. Prayer in this worldview is about aligning one's self to the existing plan, not about changing the way things are or could be.

Free-will thinking says that anything is possible, we just have to figure out how to do it. This is helpful in making positive changes, both personally and corporately; but it is negative when a person is shamed or blamed into taking responsibility for what is beyond them.

Another unhelpful characteristic that both worldviews share is blaming God for things we do not like, instead of looking for the way God is

145

acting and interacting to bring healing and wholeness out of the situation. Many times people blame God for things that can actually be traced to people. Examples include the fact that people build in unstable areas of the natural world, then blame God for fires and floods. People hoard and waste and fight over things, then blame God for hunger and a lack of clean water. This blaming behavior is not helpful as it neither provides a correct explanation, nor does it inspire people to change their behavior.

ChristoPagan thought on prayer, based on the theology presented thus far, is that prayer is aligning ourselves to God's desired best outcome and in doing so learning to live beyond ourselves in communion with God, each other, and the world. In this system, the traditional Christian modes of prayer can be blended with Pagan understandings in order to provide meaning and peace to practitioner's lives. More details on the 'how' of this blending at the end of this chapter.

Separate but connected to prayer, meditation is regulated and focused in Christianity in ways very different from Eastern religions. Rather than focusing on emptying the mind of thoughts, Christian meditation takes a verse or phrase from the Bible; or an image of Christ or the saints, and holds it as the central thought-process until the cognitive leap is made from that word or image to the Divine love at the heart of all. The Rosary is, in fact, a form of meditation that has been given a central place in the Catholic church and which has taken on most of the structure of a Sacrament. Other forms of meditation include reciting the Creeds or Psalms, *lectio divina* (a four step process for meditating), and guided meditations using the Bible, devotionals, or other materials.[lxxx] All of these methods share a desire to connect the believer to God through the use of words and symbols from the Christian tradition.

Energy, in Christianity, is the Holy Spirit at work. Humans do not have special abilities of their own for healing or the changing of circumstances, whatever positive things happen in life are the result of the Holy Spirit. There is not a sense that people have energy fields around them, nor that there are good or bad personal energies. The closest Christianity gets to these Pagan ideas is in the idea of gifts; that is, special talents that believers are given by the Holy Spirit for the work of spreading the faith and sustaining the faithful. Based on various Bible passages that discussed the ministries of the early church, the idea that there are spiritual gifts which make each believer unique is very common across denominations.[lxxxi]

As psychological understandings make their way into church life, discussion of 'toxic' people and so forth are becoming more common, but this is not an inherently Christian way to discuss it. Historically, positive energy was from the Holy Spirit and negative energy was from Satan, and depending on the era and the church, these two were sometimes considered locked in a deadly dualism, the outcome of which was certain overall, but not certain for the individual. This is not the dominant view today, although 'evil spirits' or 'demonic possession' remain on the books in some churches and are preached and taught in others. By and large, however, negative energy is seen by the Mainline churches as psychological in nature, not as manifesting the power of evil entities.

- The "traditional" Pagan understanding

The closest Pagans get to a traditional understanding is that most believe in magick. Often spelled with a 'k' to distinguish from slight-of-hand tricks (and frankly because it looks more archaic and therefore cooler), magick is the belief that human beings can use the power of their personal selves to change the outcome of events. Perhaps one of the more misunderstood elements of Paganism, magick goes back to the ancient practices of early religion. In the Bible, and throughout the ancient world, there exist a wide variety of rituals and practices to help the crops grow, ensure fertility, and aid healing (as well as curse others, cause harm, and prevent good from coming to enemies). Often these were what is known as sympathetic magic, that is, the practice of doing something on a small scale meant to encourage something on a larger scale. Much of this magick revolved around fertility rites, since if the crops did not grow people starved, and if the women did not have lots of children the tribe would be overrun. The magick was usually done in one of two ways. First, people could propitiate the spirits or gods of the land to keep them from doing something bad; or they could ask for something good. Some fantastic books on early religious magick can be found in the Suggested Reading; but the important thing for now is to know that in ancient magick it was all about people interacting with the gods or spirits they believed in to cause effects in the physical world.

Fast forward to the modern era and the beginning of what is now called New Age thought. The rituals and Magick used by these Neopagans is still often associated with the gods and spirits a practitioner worships, but there is now a belief that individuals possess a kind of personal energy which can be used either to aid the divine supplication, or that can even be used independently from a divine supplication. Any basic book on Paganism will most likely include an entire section on magick, usually with elaborate correspondences and symbolism deemed necessary for the most advantageous workings. Whether a deity is involved or not, the idea is that focused intention can produce tangible results. Scientific studies on prayer and magick are conflicted, a lot of it seems to be the powerful psychology of self-fulfilling prophecy; but then again there are other studies that imply there might be more to it than just a placebo effect.[lxxxii] Either way, for many Pagan practitioners the use of magick is one of the characteristic hallmarks of their faith.

Meditation, whether the Eastern style of emptying the mind or the Western style of focusing thought, is commonly practiced within Paganism of all kinds. Meditation is generally considered a beneficial spiritual practice and is encouraged, whether or not the particular tradition has a specific way to engage in it.

Energy is, as we have seen, considered to be a both-and proposition in Paganism. Humans can both connect to divine energy and they have a sort of internal battery that can be used as well to power positive results. Entire world-views have developed around the manipulation of energy and energy fields, and many quasi-religious practices make the claim to utilize personal or divine energy for everything from healing to making money. Paganism is usually much more liberal about tolerating these claims than other faiths, although Paganism is also more likely to give scientific evidence more weight, an inherent contradiction that the faiths comprising Paganism have not yet managed to resolve. Given that Christianity, with its larger population and greater resources, has not resolved the faith-science dilemma either; only time will tell how the various ideas around energy working will be resolved.

- The arguments against blending the Christian and Pagan understandings

The arguments against blending Christian and Pagan understandings are quite varied, and depend on the particular theology used by each. In general, Christians are leery of the idea that people can make a positive impact through the use of non-material energies, although very few

Christians would not allow for the possibility of supernatural intervention that defies explanation. In general, Pagans are more receptive of the idea that there are ways of being beyond the current understanding of science, and that focused mental energy can and does have an impact in the world. In both cases, concerns need to be raised about charlatans and cult type leaders; and in both there is a fine line between fatalism and free will that needs to be walked. While theologically subtle, perhaps the largest difference between the two religions is whether or not humans are capable of good outside of divine intervention; a quandary rendered unnecessary by the theology presented in this work.

- Suggested theology for blending Christian and Pagan understandings

Prayer is agreed on by both religions as a vital way of connecting to the Divine. The means and methods of prayer detailed above are commonly used by both faiths, all that differs is the divine person(s) to whom the prayers are directed. As the discussion of God detailed, there

153

is not an inherent conflict between God images since God is love. Therefore, whatever is loving is God and whatever is not loving is 'sin' in the sense of missing the mark, or failing to live into the best possible future that God is calling us all to. Prayer is seen by both as a multifaceted tool for spiritual growth that includes praise, thanks, intercession, and contrition within its boundaries.

Magick, that is, the intentional focus of energy to achieve a desired result, can be likened to a kind of intercession that offers up the energy of the person praying as a kind of sacrifice. While in Christian thought Christ is the ultimate sacrifice, the idea of austerity or sacrifice granting merit is historically a part of Christianity as well as other religions. The monastics gave up much in pursuit of God, and in doing so, many of them were counted as miracle workers. Even the most humble of believers can aid others through intercessory prayer; magick seems to be a ritualized form of intercession when divine aspects are invoked. Caution must always be taken to not attempt to force a certain result, the universe is bigger than we are and we cannot know all the outcomes of a given action. Both Pagan and Christian agree on this point, whether it is called magick or prayer, both faiths teach that we may ask, but we have to take no for an answer as well. Why? In part because what we are asking for might not actually be in our best interest, and in part because everyone involved has free will. God can and does lure us, woo us, plead with us to do what is right...but the final earthly decision is ours in this theology.[lxxxiii] As such, there is always the possibility that things will not turn out as we want them to.

The best spiritual practice for magick or intercession is thus to draw near to God, and having done whatever one can to promote love, trust in God for the final outcome. Note here that "we" is way bigger than you-and-I. There are over 6 billion people on the planet, each one trying to create a best outcome for themselves. It would be hubris to say that I create my reality when, in fact, I can only contribute to the creating of reality (since everyone else, and everything else, plays a role as well).

Energy is understood as the power of intention, something that science is beginning to understand but which is always larger than the individual due to the fact that the divine moves in and through all things. Connecting to this infinite energy is the object of most religious practice, and realizing the extent to which we 'live and move and have our being' within this infinite energy is in many ways a sign of enlightenment or *theosis*.[lxxxiv]

At the end of the day, our lives will have good and bad; things we can control and things we cannot change. Our emotional response to all of these is conditioned by the extent to which we feel we are in harmony with God and the universe; something which is in turn conditioned by how deeply and routinely we engage in our religious practice. Thus, the practice of the religious life is critical for our own spiritual and emotional well-being, in addition to being an effective way to celebrate our understandings of life.

Wheel of the Year

The wheel of the year is a Pagan concept that celebrates the natural cycle of the northern hemisphere, along with additional festivals drawn from the western (mainly British) culture where much of modern Paganism began. Various Reconstructionist groups have their own holy days, and this section might not apply to ChristoPagans seeking to blend Christian practice with a specific branch of Paganism. However, for more Wiccan or Eclectic rooted ChristoPagans, this calendar should work well.

This section is different from the others in that all I present here are brief descriptions of the combined major holy days, rather than all the varied perspectives and theologies. Primarily this is because the rituals themselves are where the theology will take place, and I am writing an entire book on ChristoPagan rituals which will go into depth on the theology for each holy day. That book will be a companion to this one and is expected to be out by the end of 2016.

Yule/ Christmas (Dec 21/25)

This is one of the two most important days in the blended ChristoPagan calendar. As the solstice, it celebrates the return of light into the darkness of winter. As Christmas it celebrates the birth of the Light of God. Given that the Christian festival was created out of the Pagan events of this season, there is much overlap with the celebration, keeping light and hope as central themes.

Imbolc (Feb 2)

This festival celebrates the births happening in the livestock that would keep farmers going for another year. It is also deeply associated with Brigid, the Celtic Goddess of smiths, fire, and crafting. She was so popular that she became syncretized into Christianity as St. Brigid, and as the patroness of crafters her feast day is interwoven here. In many ways Brigid is also the patron of ChristoPagans, since She is both goddess and saint, Pagan and Christian.

Lent

Beginning 40 days before Easter, excluding Sundays, this is a time to reflect on what is holding you back from God, and to engage in study, sacrifice, and other acts of change.

Ostara/ Easter (Varies)

The spring equinox marks another turn of the season, and is the highest holy day in the Christian calendar. The resurrection of Jesus, the triumph of his message of love and peace despite the power of human oppression, is celebrated here by the return of all life from the cold clutches of winter.

Beltane (May 1) and Pentecost (50 days after Easter)

This holiday celebrates the fertility of the land and of people, and depending on the year it might fall close to Pentecost, which is the Christian festival of the beginning of the Church.

Midsummer (around June 20)

The longest day of the year, it celebrates the light even as it acknowledges the return of the darkness.

Lammas (Aug 1)

First of three harvest festivals. Festival of grain and harvest, celebrated with fresh bread. Another syncretic celebration, adopted by the Christian church when it took over Celtic lands.

Mabon (around Sept 21)

Second of three harvest festivals. Celebrated at the autumn equinox when light and dark are in perfect balance, it also celebrates the ingathering of fruit and other harvest items, in preparation for the winter.

Samhain (Oct 31)

Last of the harvest festivals, often when animals were killed and prepared for storage through the winter. Historically a time when the living and the dead were closest, and a variety of ancestor rituals took place alongside the harvest celebrations. All Souls Eve and All Saint's Day are the Christianized versions of these celebrations.

Advent (40 days before Christmas, including Sundays)

This is a reverential season in preparation for the birth of Christ. It is a season of expectation, hope, and celebration.

Minor holy days

Throughout the Christian world there are any number of feast days, celebrations, and sacramental occasions depending on the time and culture. While the days above are all historical festivals celebrated by Christians and Pagans, and that form the main holy days of both faiths, there is no reason why ChristoPagans cannot celebrate other holy days as well. Many churches or covens celebrate their founding day, others celebrate the feast day of their patron saints or deity figures.

One such day that seems very appropriate is the Feast of St. Francis, held on Oct 4. As the Christian patron saint of animals and ecology, he offers an important Christian example of caring for the earth. Traditionally animals are brought and blessed during this service, thanking them for their presence in our lives and asking God to watch over them in the year to come.

This is one example of a "lesser" feast that could be given greater place in a ChristoPagan gathering, and the ritual calendars of Catholic, Orthodox, or Anglican churches offer hundreds more saintly examples; while local cultures might add celebrations important to their understanding of who they are as a community.

Beginning and the End

In the beginning of this book I claimed that to be Christian you had to take Jesus and the Bible seriously, while to be a Pagan you had to take the Earth and the divine Feminine seriously. As syncretic practitioners, ChristoPagans seek to hold the important core of both faiths, and I hope that this initial foray into ChristoPagan theology has offered ideas and insights for how serious, devoted people can deepen their spiritual growth while claiming both religious traditions as their own. This is just the beginning of ChristoPagan theology, not the end.

Amen, and Blessed Be.

Suggested Reading

There are tens of thousands of books on these subjects. These are authors that I personally have read or that come highly recommended by people I trust. None are explicitly ChristoPagan, but all have insights to offer. Many of these will be available through Inter-library Loan or at your local seminary library, some of which are open to the public. In many places I have listed major authors rather than individual books, since some of these figures are seminal in the field listed and as such all of their work has value.

Beginning Christianity

Bilezekian, Gilbert. *Christianity 101*. This is more fundamentalist and Calvinist that I would ever espouse, but it gives a basic idea of what is being taught in churches around the country.

Borg, Marcus. Everything he has written. He is Protestant, and writes in such a readable way that even convoluted things make sense. Reading from earlier to recent writings he is very honest about his Christian journey and the search for meaning that blends rational and mystical.

Wills, Gary. Everything he has written. He is another fabulous scholar, difference is that he is Catholic and so deals with issues facing that branch of Christianity.

Beginning Paganism

Adler, Margot. *Drawing Down the Moon* is a combination ethnography and guide. Harder to read than some others, but it is a classic for a reason. Her 20th anniversary edition was published shortly before her death and was a much needed update of the original.

Buckland, Raymond. He wrote on different kinds of Paganism, considered by folks I know to be dated, but his works still gave me a lot of information in the beginning.

Cunningham, Scott. His *Wicca for the Solitary Practitioner* is a classic, and while many other works have come since then, it is a solid read for anyone wanting to understand Wiccan practice. His other works vary in quality, depending on how enamored of macigk you are.

Higginbotham, Joyce & River. They have several books including one on ChristoPaganism. *Disclaimer: I know them, so I chose not to read their book on ChristoPaganism in order to keep from inadvertently borrowing anything. I recommend their work, especially since they have a very different perspective than mine, and because they are long time members of the Pagan community.*

Lale, Erin. *Asatru for Beginners.*

Paxson, Diana. *Essential Asatru.*

Starhawk. She is more radical and angry than I am, but her work defined much of early Paganism in America and still has considerable influence.

http://www.erichshall.com/asanew/bblist.htm has a Heathen list for beginners, mostly historical works.

Bible Word Studies

Balz, Horst. and Schneider, Gerhard, eds. *Exegetical Dictionary of the New Testament.*

Bauer, Walter. *A Greek-English Lexicon of the New Testament and Other Early Christian Literature*; 2nd ed.

Botterweck, G. Johannes and Ringgren, Helmer, eds. *Theological Dictionary of the Old Testament.* 8 vols.

Brown, Colin, ed. *The New International Dictionary of New Testament Theology*

Harris, R. Laird, Archer, Gleason L., and Waltke, Bruce K. eds. *Theological Wordbook of the Old Testament.*

Jenni, Ernst, and Westermann, Claus, eds. *Theological Lexicon of the Old Testament.*

Kittel, Gerhard, and Friedrich, Gerhard, eds. *Theological Dictionary of the New Testament*

Koehler, Ludwig, and Baumgartner, Walter, eds. *Lexicon in Veteris Testamenti Libros.*

Spicq, Ceslas. *Theological Lexicon of the New Testament.* Trans. and ed. James D. Earnest.

VanGemeren, Willem, ed. *The New International Dictionary of Old Testament Theology and Exegesis.* 5 vols.

Biblical Interpretation

Gorman, Michael J. *Scripture: An Ecumenical Introduction to the Bible and its Interpretation*

____ *Elements of Biblical Exegesis: A Basic Guide for Students and Ministers*

Pelikan, Jaroslav *Whose Bible is it? A Short History of the Scriptures.* London: Penguin Press, 2005.

Anything by Walter Brueggemann, Gary Wills, N.T. Wright, or Marcus Borg.

The New Interpreter's Study Bible is packed with scholarly insights, as is the *New Oxford Annotated Bible.*

The *Interpretation* bible commentary series is very useful, you can buy it as a set or just for specific books.

The New Interpreter's Bible One-Volume Commentary is a great start for people. There is also a 12-volume set (very expensive) which is much more expansive, but this one-volume commentary gives a good grounding. **If you can only get one commentary, get this one.**

Celtic Christianity

http://english.glendale.cc.ca.us/christ.h tml site is full of great reading on Celtic Christianity.

A.M. Allchin, *Praise Above All*, University of Wales Press, Cardiff, 1991.

Bradley, Ian, *The Celtic Way*, Darton, Longman and Todd, London, 1993.

Carmichael, Alexander. *Carmina Gadelica*, Lindisfarne Press, 1992.

Davies, Oliver, trans. and ed. *Celtic Spirituality*. New York: Paulist Press, 1999.

de Waal, Esther. *The Celtic Way of Prayer*, Doubleday, 1997.

Earle, Mary and Maddox, Sylvia *Praying with the Celtic Saints*, Saint Mary's Press, Winona, Minnesota, 2000.

Mackey, James P. *An Introduction to Celtic Christianity*, T and T Clark, Edinburgh, 1995

Newell, Philip *Listening for the Heartbeat of God*, Paulist Press, 1997.

O' Donoghue, Noel. *The Mountain Behind the Mountain*, T and T Clark, Edinburgh, 1993

O'Donohue, John. *Anamcara*, Harper Collins, New York, 1997.

Sheldrake, Philip *Living Between Worlds*, Cowley Publications, Boston, 1995

Chants and Songs (Pagan)

http://www.en-chant-ment.ca/

http://www.earthspirit.com/mtongue/chtlib/chtlifr.html

Christian History

Pelikan, Jaroslav. *The Christian Tradition.* Multi-volume set. Dry as dust in places, but has more information packed into a small space than any other history I have read.

Gonzalez, Justo. *The story of Christianity.* Multi-volume set.

Posnov, Mikhail. From the Orthodox point of view.

Christian Universalism

Gulley, Philip & Mulholland, James. They have written several books together and separately. *If Grace is True, If God is Love,* and *If the Church were Christian* are all fabulous books I devoured.

Creation/Earth Spirituality

Berry, Thomas. *The Great Work*

----- *The Dream of the Earth*

Fox, Matthew. Founder of much of Creation Spirituality, all his books offer insight into his blend of Christianity and ecological spirituality.

Gottlieb, Roger. *This Sacred Earth.* Not explicitly Christian, but offers perspectives from various religions on the intersection between faith and ecology.

Ruether, Rosemary R. *Gaia and God* is an ecofeminist manifesto.

Cyber Hymnal (Christian)

http://www.cyberhymnal.org/

Process Theology

www.processandfaith.org is a fantastic website with more info on Process Theology.

All books by:

       Cobb, John

       Griffin, David Ray

       Suhocki, Marjorie

       Whitehead, Alfred North (founder)

Progressive Christianity

http://www.faithandreason.org/

www.tcpc.org

www.progressivechristianity.net

Armstrong, Karen. I don't always agree with her writing, but she always makes me think.

Pagels, Elaine. She writes theology and history.

https://en.wikipedia.org/wiki/Progressive_Christianity has a great list of Progressive Christian authors, including links to their wiki sites and/or webpages for more info. A lot of the other authors references in this suggested reading, such as Marcus Borg and Phillul Gulley, fit here as well.

Paganism, Traditions

www.witchvox.com Witches' Voice is a fabulous site with hundreds of resources including finding people in your area. Each tradition usually has a website and organization attached, and this site provides a usually well tracked way to keep up with Pagan groups.
http://www.witchvox.com/_x.html?c=trads is the direct link to the various traditions they reference.

Publishers, Christian

Abingdon Press. United Methodist, ranges from fundamentalist to very liberal.

Augsberg Fortress. Lutheran, generally conservative but some good progressive books creep in from time to time.

Beacon Press. Unitarian Universalist, extremely liberal.

Beacon Hill Press. Church of the Nazarene. Very conservative.

Brazos Press. Conservative.

College Press. Very conservative.

Church publishing/ Morehouse. Episcopalian. Ranges from liberal to very conservative.

Group Publishers. Very conservative.

Pilgrim Press. United Church of Christ. Very liberal with some conservative on the edges.

W.B. Eerdmans. Reformed / Calvinist. More conservative than not.

Westminster John Knox. Reformed/ Presbyterian. Generally conservative although some slip through that are more open.

Zondervan (also uses HarperCollins). Largest Christian publisher, generally very conservative.

Publishers, Pagan

Llewellyn is the largest, but IMHO they publish a lot of "buyer beware" quality books in addition to solid work.

Amazon.com and Barnes & Noble both have self-publishing divisions and a lot of new materials are coming from these and other self-published sources, rather than more established channels. This makes it hard to determine the content, quality, or perspective of Pagan books in the same way that Christian publishers offer. My best advice is if you find an author that is helpful, read their references and suggested reading to get an idea for where to go next.

Appendix One: The Rosary and other Prayers

This appendix has a simple layout, with the traditional prayers first, then my ChristoPagan adaptations, along with my theological justifications for the changes.

Apostle's Creed (Traditional)

I believe in God, the Father Almighty, Creator of heaven and earth; and in Jesus Christ, God's only Son, our Lord; Who was conceived by the Holy Spirit, born of the Virgin Mary, suffered under Pontius Pilate, was crucified, died, and was buried. He descended into hell; the third day He arose again from the dead. He ascended into heaven, and sits at the right hand of God, the Father Almighty; from thence He shall come to judge the living and the dead. I believe in the Holy Spirit, the Holy Catholic Church, the communion of Saints, the forgiveness of sins, the resurrection of the body and life everlasting. Amen.

Creeds are not my favorite meditation tool, so I tend to omit this rather than say it at the beginning of the Rosary. It is more of a historical affirmation than a modern statement of devotion, so it is up to individuals how or if they would want to include or adapt this.

Glory Be (Traditional)

Glory be to the Father, and to the Son, and to the Holy Spirit. As it was in the beginning, is now, and ever shall be, world without end. Amen.
This reinforces Trinitarian theology. Any ChristoPagans who are also Trinitarian in nature and wish to use this prayer can substitute out their preferred names for God. An example is below.

Glory Be (Adapted)

Glory be to God, and to the Christ, and to the Holy Spirit. As it was in the beginning, is now, and ever shall be, world without end. Amen.

Hail Mary (Traditional)

Hail Mary, full of grace, the Lord is with thee; blessed art thou among women, and blessed is the

fruit of thy womb, Jesus. Holy Mary, Mother of God,
pray for us sinners, now and at the hour of our
death. Amen.

This prayer is very medieval in the focus on death
and sin. By changing three words, it goes from
dour to delightful, and fits both Christian and
ChristoPagan theology.

Hail Mary (Adapted)

Hail Mary, full of grace, the Lord is with thee;
blessed art thou among women, and blessed is the
fruit of thy womb, Jesus. Holy Mary, Mother of God,
pray for your children, now and at the hour of our
trial. Amen.

Our Father (Traditional)

Our Father, who art in heaven, hallowed be Thy
name; Thy kingdom come; Thy will be done on
earth as it is in heaven. Give us this day our daily
bread; and forgive us our trespasses as we forgive
those who trespass against us; and lead us not into
temptation; but deliver us from evil. Amen.

Our Father (Adapted- Simple)

Our Father and Mother, who art in heaven, hallowed be Thy name; Thy kingdom come; Thy will be done on earth as it is in heaven. Give us this day our daily bread; and forgive us our trespasses as we forgive those who trespass against us; and lead us not into temptation; but deliver us from evil. Amen. This prayer is rather Heaven-centric, and seems to imply that God can tempt, which I disagree with. However, this is the easiest adaptation, being simply one of gender balance. The next adaptation is my personal prayer, but it isn't as close to the Scriptural original.

Beloved One (Our Father Adapted- Complex)

Beloved One, who dwells throughout the Universe, hallowed be Thy name. Thy kingdom come; Thy will be done. Give us this day our daily bread; and forgive us our trespasses as we forgive those who trespass against us. Deliver us from evil. Amen.

The Sinner's Prayer (Traditional)

Lord Jesus Christ, son of God, have mercy on me, a
sinner.

Again, the dour tone is very present. However, this
prayer is a wonderful calming breath prayer,
breathing in on the first half and exhaling on the
second half.[lxxxv] Changing two words keeps the
breath rhythm but makes the theology more
welcoming.

The Sinner's Prayer (Adaped)

Lord Jesus Christ, Son of God, have mercy on me,
your child.

i   Pew Research: http://pewresearch.org/pubs/1616/american-marriage-interracial-interethnic bears this out.

ii Many Asatru prefer the term "Heathen" to distinguish themselves from other forms of Paganism. For the purposes of this work, the term Pagan is used for all faiths which seek to honor the Earth and the Divine Feminine; even as I fully acknowledge there are lots and lots of differences between all the branches. By necessity this is an overview work, so some things are oversimplified.

iii

http://www.patheos.com/blogs/allergicpagan/2014/09/04/what-is-humanisticnaturalistic-paganism/

iv Called the "Wesleyan quadrilateral", it was developed by a theologian named Albert Outler. See here for more: https://en.wikipedia.org/wiki/Wesleyan_Quadrilateral

v   http://religions.pewforum.org/reports

vi See the Catholic Catechism located at http://www.vatican.va/archive/ENG0015/_INDEX.HTM

vii For example the church has seen as heretical Arianism (Jesus is created by God); Modalism (God is One and acts in three modes, much like I might be Wife, Mommy, and Friend); and Unitarianism (God is One not Three). All three of these were based on biblical interpretations and all three exist today to one extent or another in various churches.

viii The Catholic Church believes it is the vehicle for the Holy Spirit, while Charismatic churches believe the individual

believer is the vehicle. See
http://www.vatican.va/archive/ENG0015/__PK.HTM for
the Catholic view, and one such Charismatic church is the
Assembly of God denomination, http://ivalue.ag.org/

ix The Catholic pro-*filioque* argument:
http://www.newadvent.org/cathen/06073a.htm. One example
of the Orthodox side of the argument:
http://malankaraorthodoxchurch.in/index.php?option=com_c
ontent&task=view&id=104&Itemid=217

x Asatru is a Pagan religion which focuses on the Norse
pantheon and its rituals. For a basic primer see *Essential
Asatru: Walking the Path of Norse Paganism* by Paxon,
Diana L. I found http://www.runestone.org/ and
http://www.thetroth.org/ to have good information. I have
had little contact with Asatru practitioners, and as such they
will not be given a great deal of focus in this work. I fully
acknowledge they are part of the Pagan/Heathen community,
but my Path has led in a different way, and as such I am
writing what I know, with no offense meant to their
tradition.

xi Fortune, Dion; Knight, Gareth (30 June 2003). The Sea
Priestess.
http://books.google.com/books?id=uZl4DKIB5WoC&pg=P
P1. Her famous line "All gods are one god, and all goddesses
are one goddess, and there is one initiator" is quoted often by
Wiccans and others in the 'soft' camp.

xiii Fundamentalism can be understood as "A movement or

183

attitude stressing strict and literal adherence to a set of basic principles" (Mirriam-Webster) http://www.merriam-webster.com/netdict/fundamentalist accessed 6/2/2010

xiv A source for feminine references to God in the Bible: http://clubs.calvin.edu/chimes/970418/o1041897.htm. An introduction to early church sources regarding the Spirit as feminine: http://www.pistissophia.org/The_Holy_Spirit/the_holy_spirit.html. For more academic works, see Suggested Reading.

xv A site with very solid details on the issues of textual criticism is http://www.crivoice.org/index.html

xvi Matt. 13:1-9; Luke 15:8-10; Matt 23:37; Deut. 32:4

xvii Some Pagans already do this to some degree, but I am going farther, incorporating Christian and Pagan doctrines into a syncretic whole, which is different from adding Jesus or Mary to an otherwise totally Pagan outlook. This adding of Christian doctrine to religious practice is what I believe makes ChristoPagans distinct from other Pagans who may include Mary, Jesus, etc. in the list of worshiped deities.

xviii I owe a debt to my seminary professors who tried so hard to hammer the doctrine of the Trinity into my head. I still don't understand how we can claim to know God's fullness. Instead, the approach I am presenting here is one way I can understand what God is like, which may or may not have anything to do with what God is really like.

xix For example, "Divine Likeness: Toward a Trinitarian Anthropology of the Family" by Ouellet, Marc; and "The Divine Family: The Trinity and Our Life in God" by

McDonough, William K.

xx Catholic theology uses this to explain why women may not be priests: Canon Law 1024 says that "A baptized male alone receives sacred ordination validly" http://www.vatican.va/archive/ENG1104/_P3P.HTM. See also http://www.newadvent.org/library/docs_jp02os.htm which says that the church "...has imitated Christ in choosing only men..."

xxi One example of this view is found in "Women and the Word" by Schneiders, Sandra M.

xxii   John 1:1; Mark 1:1; Titus 1:4; and Isa 9:6 are verses used to justify these titles among others.

xxiii   See http://www.religioustolerance.org/chr_atone5.htm for a good group of articles on the subject.

xxiv   http://www.religioustolerance.org/chr_atone17.htm.

xxv   John 4:42; Acts 4:12; Acts 13:23; Philippians 3:20; 2 Timothy 1:10; Titus 1:4; Titus 2:13; Titus 3:6; 2 Peter 1:11; 2 Peter 2:20; 2 Peter 3:18; 1 John 4:14 among many verses proclaim this creedal statement.

xxvi   From Encyclopaedia Britannica http://www.britannica.com/EBchecked/topic/253196/hamartia

xxvii   A solid example of a theologian exploring the fear/shame paradigm is Rev. Dr. Thandecka, in her book "Learning to be White".

xxviii   Luke 10:25-37

xxix   This depends on the definition of Pagan, of course. I doubt many Hindu people would make this claim, although

some Pagans do.
http://www.patheos.com/blogs/pantheon/2012/02/when-hinduism-confuses-and-frustrates-me/

xxx   An example is: http://www.krishna.com/node/118

xxxi   For an understanding of why Universalism seems to be the most logical and loving option to me with regard to salvation, see *If Grace is True* and *If Love is True* both by Gulley and Mulholland.

xxxii   Acts 9:31 for example.

xxxiii One website with good info on Montanus among others is http://www.earlychurch.org.uk/montanism.php

xxxiv   Luke 10:25-37

xxxv   Even Catholic theology staunchly defends this communion of the Trinity: "For as the Trinity has only one and the same natures so too does it have only one and the same operation..." Catechism of the Catholic Church #258 http://www.scborromeo.org/ccc/p1s2c1p2.htm#I

xxxvi   Albeit in a minority position, but 2,000 years of theological development means that She DOES exist within the tradition of the church, and as such is not a heretical new development. Theology that still sees the Spirit as feminine: http://www.luminarium.org/medlit/julian.htm (Julian of Norwich); http://www.theology.edu/journal/volume3/spirit.htm (R.P. Nettelhorst, theologian at a Southern Baptist school), note that the ideas of what constitutes a "feminine" place in the Trinity in this article makes my feminist blood boil. It is included here only because it shows that even in the most fundamentalist traditions, She can be found.

xxxvii   For many Mary is the Mother Goddess. Traditional theology denied that because atonement theories needed Jesus to be fully human; yet the Catholic church has given her titles and credit far beyond normal humanity (Queen of the Universe, for example). As such and with the new understanding of sin and atonement presented here, it is entirely possible for someone to see Mary and Jesus as *avatara* together.

xxxviii   A fantastic site with tons of details about Bible interpretation and study: http://www.crivoice.org/inerrant.html. I highly recommend this for more depth and detail than can be given to the subject here.

xxxix   Ex 22:18 KJV (Public Domain) see http://www.religioustolerance.org/wic_bibl2.htm

xl   Gal 5:19-20 KJV (Public Domain)

xli   See http://www.religioustolerance.org/chr_vers1.htm

xlii   http://www.soulforce.org/article/homosexuality-bible-gay-christian

xliii   http://gbgm-umc.org/umw/bible/jc.html and associated pages give a decent introduction to the history of biblical interpretation.

xliv

http://www.bigissueground.com/atheistground/cauthen-bibleinterpret.shtml is a good introduction to the liberal side; anything written by Ratzinger is a good example of the conservative side.

xlv See Lev. 17 and 18.

xlvi   *The Lucifer Effect* by Philip Zimbardo is a great analysis of how we label people in order to feel secure.

xlvii   Site has lots of good book references: http://english.glendale.cc.ca.us/christ.html

xlviii https://en.wikipedia.org/wiki/Kaaba#History

xlix   See for example the conservative theology presented here http://www.leaderu.com/orgs/probe/docs/ecology.html or http://www.christiantoday.com/article/dominion.over.the.earth.comes.with.responsibility.christians.learn/25635.htm

l   Www.witchvox.com a huge clearing house site for Pagans of many kinds.

li   See Ruether, Rosmary Radford "What is Creation Spirituality" located at http://theoblogical.org/dlature/itseminary/creaspir/whatis1.html. Also the writings of Matthew Fox.

lii   This section inspired by the works of Carol Christ, John B. Cobb, Jr., and Marjorie Suchocki, among others. For more information see www.processandfaith.org or www.ctr4process.org both of which are hubs of Process Theology. Also see Suggested Reading.

liii 1 Cor. 3:16

liv In fact, Calvin's views were much more subtle and nuanced, but this is the sense of much of later Calvinism. An example is: http://www.reformedtheology.ca/calvin.html

lv   See www.witchvox.com for more information.

lvi   Rives, James Boykin, 'Human Sacrifice Among Pagans and

Christians', Journal of Roman Studies 85 (1995) 65-85

lvii The "Left Behind" series of books is a great example of this kind of theology, usually based on totally misreading the book of Revelation in the Bible.

lviii   From Encyclopaedia Britannica http://www.britannica.com/EBchecked/topic/253196/hamarti a accessed.

lix See Rev. Dr. Thandecka, in her book "Learning to be White".

lx If Grace is True is the best articulation of this Universalism I have ever read. The insights of the authors are totally applicable to ChristoPagans as well as Christians.

lxi http://www.religioustolerance.org/heav_hell.htm

lxii Origen, a great Early Church writer, believed in reincarnation. He was also condemned for heresy, although many modern scholars are more accepting of his work. Competing sites: http://reluctant-messenger.com/origen.html (esoteric Christianity) and http://www.newadvent.org/cathen/11306b.htm (Roman Catholic)

lxiii   Nice simple discussion of Pagan afterlives: http://www.patheos.com/Library/Pagan/Beliefs/Afterlife-and-Salvation.html

lxiv   Interesting site trying to blend this: http://astrology.about.com/od/thehistoryofastrology/a/christi anastro.htm

lxv http://www.religioustolerance.org/divin_bibl.htm

lxvi   http://www.jameslindlibrary.org/articles/casting-and-drawing-lots-a-time-honoured-way-of-dealing-with-uncertainty-and-for-ensuring-fairness/

lxvii

http://christianity.about.com/od/denominations/a/calvin arminian.htm basic information about the two positions.

lxviii I personally am friends with Little Fox Tarot http://littlefoxtarot.com/ and trust her ability to help me understand what the Universe/ my unconscious is telling me. So even though I rail against charlatans, and even though I am generally a skeptical person about anything that cannot be rationally interpreted, she has often helped me personally. If you do decide to work with non-traditional practitioners of any kind, do your homework and make sure they are trustworthy!

lxix   For a great list of resources debunking astrology see http://www.astrosociety.org/education/resources/pseudobib.html

lxx See http://www.orthodoxphotos.com/readings/beginning/catechumens.shtml for a summary introduction to Catchumens.

lxxi   A basic discussion of high and low church can be found here: http://www.crivoice.org/lowhighchurch.html

lxxii   For one high church view see http://www.newadvent.org/cathen/13295a.htm ; for a low church perspective see Disciples of Christ http://www.disciples.org/ these are two of the many perspectives, every church has a slightly different take on these issues.

lxxiii   For more on Donatus and the Donatist controversy, see http://www.anabaptistnetwork.com/donatists

lxxiv   For more info see http://www.womenpriests.org/ for Catholics and http://www.religioustolerance.org/femclrgy.htm for others.

lxxv   James 5:14-15

lxxvi   http://en.wikipedia.org/wiki/Prayer_in_Christianity is a good basic overview, but there are thousands of sites, some better some worse, which discuss this.

lxxvii   This is true across religious traditions, with Muslims, Jews, Hindus and Christians (among others) believing that the intention is crucial to the success of prayer.

lxxviii   http://www.scripturecatholic.com/saints.html

lxxix   Great article listing the problems with studying prayer from a scientific perspective: http://www.indianjpsychiatry.org/article.asp?issn=0019-5545;year=2009;volume=51;issue=4;spage=247;epage=253;aulast=Andrade

lxxx   A surprisingly good article on Christian meditation http://en.wikipedia.org/wiki/Christian_meditation

lxxxi   A quick search for 'Spiritual Gifts' will bring up an online inventory for almost every church and lots of parachurch organizations. While few or none of these tests have scientific validity, they are used to assess faithful for every aspect of church life, including the clergy in many churches.

lxxxii   See *lxix* for more information.

lxxxiii   Universalism would point out that the earthly outcome is *not* the final word, the eternal outcome is always in God's hands

lxxxiv   http://orthodoxwiki.org/Theosis offers an Orthodox viewpoint on the subject, while https://en.wikipedia.org/wiki/Divinization_%28Christian%29 offers more on the Western view.

lxxxv See https://gravitycenter.com/practice/breath-prayer/ for more breath prayers. These are fabulous for traffic and other times when a tiny mantra-like prayer helps calm and center you!

Made in the USA
Lexington, KY
12 May 2017